Family Limited Partnership

How to Protect Your Business and Provide for Your Children

FAMILY LIMITED PARTNERSHIP

How to Protect Your Business and Provide for Your Children

Karen Ann Rolcik
Attorney at Law

SPHINX® PUBLISHING
AN IMPRINT OF SOURCEBOOKS, INC.®
NAPERVILLE, ILLINOIS
www.SphinxLegal.com

First Edition, 2003

Published by: **Sphinx® Publishing, An Imprint of Sourcebooks, Inc.®**

Naperville Office
P.O. Box 4410
Naperville, Illinois 60567-4410
630-961-3900
Fax: 630-961-2168
www.sourcebooks.com
www.SphinxLegal.com

This publication is designed to provide accurate and authoritative information in regard to the subject matter covered. It is sold with the understanding that the publisher is not engaged in rendering legal, accounting, or other professional service. If legal advice or other expert assistance is required, the services of a competent professional person should be sought.

From a Declaration of Principles Jointly Adopted by a Committee of the American Bar Association and a Committee of Publishers and Associations

This product is not a substitute for legal advice.

Disclaimer required by Texas statutes.

Library of Congress Cataloging-in-Publication Data
Rolcik, Karen Ann.
Family limited partnership : how to protect your family business and provide for your children / by Karen Ann Rolcik.
p. cm.
ISBN 1-57248-254-0 (pbk.)
1. Family partnership--Taxation--United States--Popular works. I. Title.
KF6452.Z9 R65 2003
343.7305'32--dc21
2002153926

Printed and bound in the United States of America.
VHG Paperback — 10 9 8 7 6 5 4 3 2 1

Contents

Using Self-Help Law Books

Before using a self-help law book, you should realize the advantages and disadvantages of doing your own legal work and understand the challenges and diligence that this requires.

The Growing Trend

Rest assured that you won't be the first or only person handling your own legal matter. For example, in some states, more than seventy-five percent of divorces and other cases have at least one party representing him or herself. Because of the high cost of legal services, this is a major trend and many courts are struggling to make it easier for people to represent themselves. However, some courts are not happy with people who do not use attorneys and refuse to help them in any way. For some, the attitude is, "Go to the law library and figure it out for yourself."

We at Sphinx write and publish self-help law books to give people an alternative to the often complicated and confusing legal books found in most law libraries. We have made the explanations of the law as simple and easy to understand as possible. Of course, unlike an attorney advising an individual client, we cannot cover every conceivable possibility.

Cost/Value Analysis

Whenever you shop for a product or service, you are faced with various levels of quality and price. In deciding what product or service to buy, you make a cost/value analysis on the basis of your willingness to pay and the quality you desire.

When buying a car, you decide whether you want transportation, comfort, status, or sex appeal. Accordingly, you decide among such choices as a Neon, a Lincoln, a Rolls Royce, or a Porsche. Before making a decision, you usually weigh the merits of each option against the cost.

When you get a headache, you can take a pain reliever (such as aspirin) or visit a medical specialist for a neurological examination. Given this choice, most people, of course, take a pain reliever, since it costs only pennies; whereas a medical examination costs hundreds of dollars and takes a lot of time. This is usually a logical choice because it is rare to need anything more than a pain reliever for a headache. But in some cases, a headache may indicate a brain tumor and failing to see a specialist right away can result in complications. Should everyone with a headache go to a specialist? Of course not, but people treating their own illnesses must realize that they are betting on the basis of their cost/value analysis of the situation. They are taking the most logical option.

The same cost/value analysis must be made when deciding to do one's own legal work. Many legal situations are very straight forward, requiring a simple form and no complicated analysis. Anyone with a little intelligence and a book of instructions can handle the matter without outside help.

But there is always the chance that complications are involved that only an attorney would notice. To simplify the law into a book like this, several legal cases often must be condensed into a single sentence or paragraph. Otherwise, the book would be several hundred pages long and too complicated for most people. However, this simplification necessarily leaves out many details and nuances that would apply to special or unusual situations. Also, there are many ways to interpret most legal questions. Your case may come before a judge who disagrees with the analysis of our authors.

Therefore, in deciding to use a self-help law book and to do your own legal work, you must realize that you are making a cost/value analysis. You have decided that the money you will save in doing it yourself outweighs the chance that your case will not turn out to your satisfaction. Most people handling their own simple legal matters never have a problem, but occasionally people find that it ended up costing them more to have an attorney straighten out the situation than it would have if they had hired an attorney in the beginning. Keep this in mind if you decide to handle your own case, and be sure to consult an attorney if you feel you might need further guidance.

LOCAL RULES

The next thing to remember is that a book which covers the law for the entire nation, or even for an entire state, cannot possibly include every procedural difference of every county court. Whenever possible, we provide the exact form needed; however, in some areas, each county, or even each judge, may require unique forms and procedures. In our *state* books, our forms usually cover the majority of counties in the state, or provide examples of the type of form that will be required. In our *national* books, our forms are sometimes even more general in nature but are designed to give a good idea of the type of form that will be needed in most locations. Nonetheless, keep in mind that your *state*, county, or judge may have a requirement, or use a form, that is not included in this book.

You should not necessarily expect to be able to get all of the information and resources you need solely from within the pages of this book. This book will serve as your guide, giving you specific information whenever possible and helping you to find out what else you will need to know. This is just like if you decided to build your own backyard deck. You might purchase a book on how to build decks. However, such a book would not include the building codes and permit requirements of every city, town, county, and township in the nation; nor would it include the lumber, nails, saws, hammers, and other materials and tools you would need to actually build the deck. You would use the book as your guide, and then do some work and research involving such matters as whether you need a permit of some kind, what type and grade of wood are available in your area, whether to use hand tools or power tools, and how to use those tools.

Before using the forms in a book like this, you should check with your court clerk to see if there are any local rules of which you should be aware, or local forms you will need to use. Often, such forms will require the same information as the forms in the book but are merely laid out differently, use slightly different language, or use different color paper so the clerks can easily find them. They will sometimes require additional information.

Changes in the Law

Besides being subject to state and local rules and practices, the law is subject to change at any time. The courts and the legislatures of all fifty states are constantly revising the laws. It is possible that while you are reading this book, some aspect of the law is being changed or that a court is interpreting a law in a different way. You should always check the most recent statutes, rules and regulations to see what, if any changes have been made.

In most cases, the change will be of minimal significance. A form will be redesigned, additional information will be required, or a waiting period will be extended. As a result, you might need to revise a form, file an extra form, or wait out a longer time period; these types of changes will not usually affect the outcome of your case. On the other hand, sometimes a major part of the law is changed, the entire law in a particular area is rewritten, or a case that was the basis of a central legal point is overruled. In such instances, your entire ability to pursue your case may be impaired.

Again, you should weigh the value of your case against the cost of an attorney and make a decision as to what you believe is in your best interest.

Introduction

Each year thousands of limited partnerships are registered in this country. Limited partnerships, like corporations, offer the advantage of limited personal liability to its owners. Limited personal liability protects the assets of the owners from the creditors of the limited partnership. Unlike a corporation, a limited partnership is very flexible with regard to payments to its owners.

Limited partnerships have been used since 1916 when states first adopted the *Uniform Limited Partnership Act* (ULPA). Since adopting the ULPA, many states have enacted the Revised Uniform Limited Partnership Act (RULPA). Therefore, limited partnerships have a very long history of stability, predictability and dependability for achieving asset protection goals.

The main reason people form limited partnerships is to avoid personal liability. While sole proprietors and partners of general partnerships have their personal assets at risk, partners of limited partnerships risk only what they paid for their partnership interest. A limited partnership effectively shelters assets from the owners' creditors, lawsuit judgments, divorce and tax claims. With so many people ready to sue for any reason at all, the limited partnership is one of the few inexpensive protections left.

Many families have created limited partnerships as a way to protect and preserve wealth for present and future generations. These are called *Family Limited Partnerships*. In a typical limited partnership created by a family, the parents will be the owners of the general partnership interest in the limited partnership and will also own interests in the limited partnership. The parents will also give limited partnership interests to children and/or grandchildren. However, the parents, being general partners, will maintain control over the family's assets transferred to the limited partnership. They can, at the same time, transfer a portion of the financial benefit of the assets to children and grandchildren. Family Limited Partnerships are, therefore, an effective way to provide for your children while protecting your current assets.

Creating a simple Family Limited Partnership is very easy and the purpose of this book is to explain, in simple language, how you can do it yourself. A simple Family Limited Partnership is where there are ten or fewer partners.

If you plan to sell a partnership interest to someone who is not active in the business or who is not a family member, you should seek the advice of an attorney. However, some guidance is provided throughout this book for some of the concerns in these circumstances.

If your situation is complicated or involves factors not mentioned in this book, you should seek the advice of an attorney practicing partnership law. The cost of a short consultation can be less expensive than the consequences of violating the law.

If you plan to sell Family Limited Partnership interests to outside investors, you should consult with a lawyer who specializes in securities laws. Selling Family Limited Partnership interests equal to a few percentage points to friends and neighbors may sound like an easy way to raise capital for your business, but it is not. Since the stock market crash of the 1930's, there have been federal laws regulating the sale of securities. There are harsh criminal penalties for violators and the laws do not have many loopholes.

While this book explains the *basics* of partnership taxation, you should discuss your own particular situation with your accountant before deciding what is best for you. He or she can set up an efficient system of bookkeeping that can save both time and money.

Chapter 1 explains the basics of partnerships in general. Chapters 2 and 3 discuss the specifics of family limited partnerships, including the advantages and disadvantages.

Chapter 4 discusses the start-up procedures for Family Limited Partnerships, while Chapters 5–9 detail the day-to-day dealings of them (including dissolving the Family Limited Partnership).

To help you understand the terms used in this book, there is a glossary containing many of the italicized words in the chapters. The appendices contain a start-up checklist, state-by-state partnership specifics, sample filled-in forms, and perforated blank forms. A copy of the Uniform Limited Partnership Act is also contained in Appendix D. (Each state has adopted a version of the Uniform Limited Partnership Act which should be used as your legal guide in forming your limited partnership.)

Good luck with your new family business!

1 Partnership Basics

Before you can understand Family Limited Partnerships, you should familiarize yourself with some basic partnership concepts and terms. A *partnership* is formed when two or more people agree to carry on a business together. This agreement can be written or oral. A partnership is a legal "person," which can be created under state law. As a person, a partnership has certain rights and obligations, such as the right to do business. Human beings are *natural* persons, while limited partnerships are *legal* persons.

There are two kinds of partnerships: a *general partnership* and a *limited partnership.* A Family Limited Partnership is a type of limited partnership. There are very distinct differences between a general partnership and a limited partnership and it is helpful to understand the differences between the two.

General Partnerships versus Limited Partnerships

General Partnership

A general partnership is a partnership in which each partner has *unlimited liability* for the actions of the partnership. In effect, a general partnership is an association or group of *sole proprietors* who are in business together. The partners remain in direct control of the assets, or business, of the general partner. All partners have an equal and active role in the management of the business. The partners share equal responsibility for contributions and share profits equally.

The personal assets of a partner are at risk for the debts of the partnership. No local or state filings are required to create this type of partnership. A general partnership is different from a *corporation*, which does not come into existence until articles of incorporation are filed with the secretary of state, and different from a limited partnership, which does not come into existence until a *certificate of existence* is filed with the secretary of state.

In a general partnership, any one partner is able to bind the partnership by entering into a contract on behalf of the partnership.

Example: Smith and Jones are partners and Jones signs a contract on behalf of the partnership, Smith will be personally liable for the full amount of the contract. This is true regardless of whether Smith authorized the contract or whether he even knew the contract existed.

Because each of the partners has unlimited personal liability, a general partnership is the single most dangerous form of conducting business. A partner is not only liable for contracts entered into by other partners; each partner is also liable for the other partner's negligence. If a partner owns 10% of the partnership, he is still responsible for 100% of the partnership's obligations. However, the partner may seek contributions to pay such obligations from the other partners.

In a general partnership when one partner dies the partnership is automatically dissolved under the law. Additionally, personal creditors of a partner can disrupt the business of the partnership by forcing the liquidation of the partnership for purposes of reaching the debtor-partner's interest in the partnership.

Limited Partnerships

A limited partnership is a partnership (which includes family limited partnerships) that has a least one general partner and one or more limited partners. The same person can be a *general partner* and a *limited partner* as long as there are at least two legal persons who are partners in the partnership. The general partner is responsible for the management of the day-to-day affairs and has unlimited liability for all debts and obligations that are not fully satisfied by the partnership. Due to unlimited liability, many limited partnerships have entities such as a corporation or *limited liability company* that serve as a general partner to protect the individual participants from general partnership liabilities.

A *limited partner* is similar to the *shareholder* of a *corporation*. The only assets at risk are the assets invested by the limited partner in the limited partnership and any amounts which the partner has obligated himself to contribute under the terms of the partnership agreement. In exchange for the protection against personal liability, a limited partner may not actively participate in management. Historically, the limited partner was a "silent" partner. He did not want his identity revealed and did not want to operate the business. He simply wanted to invest in the business and receive a share of the profits.

However, a limited partner may have to vote on certain matters, just as a shareholder has a right to vote on some corporate matters. A typical limited partnership agreement may provide that a majority vote of the limited partners is necessary for the sale of assets or to remove a general partner. The PARTNERSHIP AGREEMENT, like the *bylaws of a corporation*, determines whether the limited partners can vote on these matters.

If a limited partner takes an active role in the management of the partnership, that partner may lose the limited liability protection and may be treated as a general partner.

Example: John, a limited partner, negotiates a contract with ABC corporation on behalf of the partnership. John may have liability as a general partner.

Limited partnerships were invented years ago to promote risky ventures. Prior to the use of limited partnerships or corporations, businesses faced the possibility of unlimited liability. By using a limited partnership, many people could put up a fixed sum of money for a new venture, such as a voyage to explore the new world. If the venture made money, they shared the profits. If the venture went into debt, the most they could lose was their initial investment. The limited partner is an investor who lends money to a business venture in exchange for a percentage of the profits of the business. Limited partners may retain their interest in the partnership for a specified time, until their investment plus their share of the profit has been repaid, or indefinitely.

The reasons for having a limited partnership are the same today. They allow investors to put up money for new ventures without risk of further liability. While our legal system is making more people liable for more things, the limited partnership remains one of the few innovations that has yet to be abandoned.

Partnership Terms

Before forming a limited partnership, you should be familiar with these common partnership terms, which will be used in the text.

A *partner* is a person who owns an interest in a limited partnership. A partner can be a person, trust, corporation or any other form of business organization.

The *registered agent* is the person designated by the limited partnership to receive legal papers that must be served on the limited partnership. The registered agent should be regularly available at the *registered office* of the limited partnership. The registered office can be the partnership's office or the office of the partnership's attorney or other person who is the registered agent. The registered agent must reside in the state in where the partnership is formed.

Certificate of Limited Partnership (in some states referred to as a *Certificate of Existence*) is the name of the document that is filed with the secretary of state to start the partnership. In most cases, the CERTIFICATE OF LIMITED PARTNERSHIP contains the name of the limited partnership, the address of the principal office, the name and address of the registered agent, and the name and address of the general partner. Since the CERTIFICATE OF LIMITED PARTNERSHIP is a public record, the names and addresses of the general partners will be publicly available but not the names of the limited partners.

The **Partnership Agreement** states the rules governing the structure and operation of the limited partnership. It states the purposes of the partnership, the duties of the general partners, matters on which the vote of the limited partners is required, the allocation of income, loss, expenses and credits among the partners, tax reporting procedures, admittance and withdrawal of partners, and a variety of other provisions. The **Partnership Agreement** can be as simple or complex as the partners desire.

A *general partner* may contribute money, assets, a service, or a combination of the three in return for a partnership interest. The general partner has total authority to conduct partnership business on behalf of the limited partnership. The general partner must establish an office and appoint an agent for service of process in the state in which the partnership is formed. The general partner must keep the records of the partnership in the office, must file the partnership documents with the secretary of state, file partnership tax returns, and give notice of partnership meetings.

As noted above, a general partner has unlimited personal liability. If a corporation is a general partner, its liability is limited to the assets owned by the corporation. The personal assets of the corporation's shareholders are not at risk–only their investment in the corporation. In most limited partnerships, the general partner(s) will own a relatively small percentage interest of the limited partnership. Generally, the percentage interest owned by the general partner is one or two percent.

A *limited partner* is generally not liable for the debts or obligations of the limited partnership, as long as he does not actively participate in the daily activities of the business. In fact, if a limited partner does become involved in the day-to-day affairs of the partnership, the courts may treat the limited partner as a general partner and all of the protections of limited liability fall away. The limited partner's personal assets are not at risk, but their investment in the partnership is at risk.

To avoid liability, a limited partner cannot file any formal documents with the state officials. A limited partner must be very careful with any statements he makes to third parties. A limited partner must not act in a manner that makes a third party believe that he or she has authority to bind the partnership. If he or she does, the limited partner could become personally liable not only to the third party, but also to the partnership.

If a limited partner is also an officer or director of a corporation or limited liability company that is a general partner, in any business transaction where the limited partner is involved, the limited partner should make clear that he is acting in his capacity as an officer or director of the general partner and not as a limited partner.

The limited partner may engage in the following activities without losing his limited liability:

- work as an independent contractor of the limited partnership;
- work as an employee of the limited partnership;
- work as an independent contractor of the general partner;
- work as an employee of the general partner;
- guarantee partnership debts; and,
- vote on the following:
  - dissolution of the partnership;
  - the sale, lease, exchange or pledging of partnership assets outside the ordinary course of business;
  - amendments to the partnership agreement; and,
  - changing the nature of the business.

The limited partner cannot give orders to the general partner. However, limited partners are not prohibited from giving *advice* to the general partner.

Limited partners, like shareholders of a corporation, have the right to review financial and tax records of the partnership. A limited partner also has the right to review all documents filed with the state such as organizational documents, amendments to such documents, the list of partners and their addresses, and each partner's share of the profits and losses of the partnership.

The general partner must provide the limited partner with information to complete his income tax return in a timely manner.

In addition to these common rights of limited partners, each state's partnership law will give limited partners certain rights. It is very important to be familiar with these rights under state law when forming a limited partnership.

In many Family Limited Partnerships (FLPs), certain limited partners are given rights that other limited partners are not given. Voting rights and income preference rights are among the most common rights varied among limited partners in an FLP. Typically, parents will restrict voting rights to their limited partnership interests, therefore maintaining control of the FLP.

FLPs often create different classes of limited partnership interests with regard to income distributions. For instance, parents may reserve to their limited partnership interests the right to receive the first five percent of any income earned by the FLP. These variations of basic limited partnership rules must be specifically set forth in the written partnership agreement.

2 Overview of Family Limited Partnerships

A *Family Limited Partnership* is the same legal entity as a limited partnership under state law. It is taxed in the same manner as a limited partnership for federal and state income taxes. The fact that the FLP has members of a family as its owners and may include parents, children, grandchildren, brothers, sisters, nieces, or nephews is what sets it apart from an ordinary limited partnership.

Members of the Partnership

"Ordinary" Limited Partnerships

Generally, "ordinary" limited partnerships are formed among individuals who are conducting a business together. They may have chosen a limited partnership as their business entity rather than a corporation or limited liability company.

Example: Four individuals who are not related to one another decide to start a publishing business. They want to limit their liability to their investment in the business and keep their personal assets separate and free from risk if the business is sued or does not succeed. A limited partnership is selected as the form of business entity that will operate the business and the individuals will own interests in the limited partnership, much like owning stock in a corporation.

Family Limited Partnerships

FLPs may be formed to own a family business, and members would include family members only.

Example: Parents decide to start a business, and although their children will not be actively involved in the business, the parents want the children to share in the ownership of the business. To protect their non-business assets separate and free from risk if the business is sued or does not succeed, the parents form an FLP to operate the business.

FLPs may also be formed to separate family, non-business assets from business assets or from risks associated with a parent's job or hobby.

Example 1: A father owns and operates an unincorporated business with two unrelated individuals. To protect the family's assets from the risks associated with he unincorporated business, the father forms an FLP and transfers assets such as the family residence, automobiles, investments, etc., to the FLP.

Example 2: A father is an airline pilot or has a private plane he enjoys flying. In order to protect the family's assets from the risks associated with his job, the father forms an FLP and transfers assets such as the family residence, automobiles, investments, etc.

Partnership Interest and Ownership

"Ordinary" Limited Partnerships

In an "ordinary" limited partnership, buy-sell provisions are often included. These provisions restrict sales of a partnership interest and generally require that the other partners, or the partnership itself, have the "right of first refusal." In other words, if a partner wants to sell his interest in the limited partnership and receives a valid offer from a third party, the partner must give the other partners the right to buy the interest at the same price offered by the third party. If the partners or partnership do not buy the interest, the selling partner has the right to sell the interest to the third party.

Example: Four women operate a retail gift store as a limited partnership. One woman wants to retire from the business and has found another woman who wants to buy her partnership interest. She makes an offer of $25,000 for the partnership interest. The selling partner must first give the remaining three partners the opportunity to buy her interest. If they do not purchase the partnership interest, the interest can be sold to the third party.

FAMILY LIMITED PARTNERSHIPS

In contrast, most FLPs provide that in no event can a partnership interest be transferred to any third party. This includes spouses, step-children, and the like. The partner would be entitled to transfer the partnership interest to other partners or to family members that the PARTNERSHIP AGREEMENT designates. The partner would be entitled to receive the price established by the PARTNERSHIP AGREEMENT that may not be equal to the fair market value of the partnership interest.

Example: The Smiths formed an FLP and gave each of their three children interests in the FLP. The oldest child no longer wants to keep his interest. His interest is valued at $10,000 by the PARTNERSHIP AGREEMENT, but the fair market value is $50,000. The child may sell his interest to the other partners or may make the partnership interest a gift to his own children.

FAMILY LIMITED PARTNERSHIP VERSUS "ORDINARY" LIMITED PARTNERSHIPS

An FLP generally has more restrictive rules regarding the ownership and transfer of partnership interests than a traditional limited partnership. Additionally, most FLPs restrict management to the creators of the FLP (typically parents) or to one or more individuals designated by the creators. An FLP often prevents removal or replacement of the management without approval of the creators. In contrast, "ordinary" limited partnerships generally permit the selection, replacement and removal of the management by a vote of the partners.

Yet another very important distinction between an FLP and an "ordinary" limited partnership is that the limited partnership interests that parents give to children and grandchildren are held in trusts where the children and grandchildren are beneficiaries. However, the trusts are controlled by trustees chosen by the parents. The trustees may or may not be other family members. The purpose of the trusts are to further protect the FLP interest from creditors of children and grandchildren. Additionally, because the trustees are selected by the parents, the assumption is that the trustees will be aware of and look to the parents for guidance with regard to the FLP interests.

Reasons for Creating an FLP

Family limited partnerships are formed among family members for a variety of reasons in addition to conducting a business or to protect family assets from business or job risks. Parents may want to provide for their children's future by keeping the family assets within the family. Family assets could be transferred to non-family members in the event of a divorce or personal bankruptcy. With so many second marriages and blended families, parents may want to make certain that the family assets are kept in the "bloodline." This is particularly true when family assets have been passed down from generation to generation in the past.

Another very popular reason for creating an FLP is to keep the assets out of the probate process upon the death of a family member. Each partner owns a partnership interest which is like owning stock in a corporation. The partner does not own any of the individual assets in the FLP. Therefore, when a partner dies, the business can continue to operate uninterrupted according to the terms of the partnership agreement or the assets in the FLP can continue to be invested or managed without the interference of a probate court.

Another reason to create an FLP is to reduce the amount of estate and inheritance taxes that would be paid upon the death of a partner.

Example: Parents create an FLP with the following ownership interests: Mom—35%; Dad—35%; Children—30%. The total value of the FLP is $1,000,000. When Dad dies, the value of his interest in the FLP is not $350,000. For estate and inheritance tax purposes, the value of Dad's interest may be reduced by as much as 40% (i.e. the value of Dad's interest would be $210,000) because of valuation discounts permitted by the Internal Revenue Service. If Dad owned 35% of the assets outright, the value would be $350,000 for estate and inheritance taxes.

FLPs are also formed to teach children or grandchildren how to operate the family business or manage family investments. By giving the children or grandchildren a financial interest in the FLP, an incentive is provided to encourage their participation. This is another way FLPs provide for a child's future.

Example: Parents own a home remodeling business and are nearing retirement. The business has been very profitable and continues to earn money for the family. The business is the parents' primary asset. Their eldest son has been working in the business and has expressed an interest in continuing the business after the parents retire. There are two other children.

The parents decide to create an FLP and transfer the business to the FLP and give each child an interest in the FLP. Because the son is interested in continuing the business, the parents have given him a slightly larger percentage interest than the other children as an incentive.

More reasons for forming an FLP are set forth in Appendix C. In recent years, the Internal Revenue Service has challenged the use of FLPs to reduce or eliminate estate taxes through valuation discounts. Courts have held that if there is a valid business purpose for the FLP, the valuation discounts will be honored if sufficiently proved.

An FLP will often have several business purposes such as asset protection, estate tax savings, avoidance of probate, involvement of children or grandchildren, or management of the FLP. When drafting the **Partnership Agreement** for an FLP, it is important to include as many business purposes as applicable. A simple statement that the FLP is formed to engage in any business permitted by state law is generally insufficient to withstand challenge by the Internal Revenue Service.

3

Pros and Cons of Family Limited Partnerships

Prior to forming a legal entity through which to operate a business, business owners should evaluate the advantages and disadvantages of the type of various legal entities. Following are some of the advantages and disadvantages of an FLP. Only after evaluating the advantages and disadvantages can a business owner make an informed decision with regard to creating an FLP.

ADVANTAGES

The following are some of the advantages that an FLP has over other forms of business, such as a *sole proprietorship* and *general partnership*.

Limited Liability of Partners

Perhaps the reason for forming a family limited partnership most often given is to limit the liability of the owners. The liability of the partners is restricted to their investment or ownership interest in the FLP. In contrast, a business conducted as a sole proprietorship or general partnership exposes the personal assets of the business owners to the debts and liabilities of the business. If the business experiences financial trouble or if the business is sued, creditors can try to collect any or all of the owners' personal assets. The creditors are not limited to the business assets.

In contrast, when an FLP that is operated correctly and the rules applicable to limited partnerships are followed, the partners' personal assets are protected from creditors. If the business of the FLP fails, the partners only lose their investment in the FLP and not their personal assets. One exception to this liability limitation is if the partners personally guarantee any debt or financial obligation of the FLP.

Example 1: Five individuals work together in a general partnership. One partner enters into a lease for office space in the name of the general partnership without the approval of the other partners. Because the partner was acting in the name of the partnership, the other partners will be held personally liable for lease payments.

If the general partnership defaults on the lease, the landlord may seek payments directly from the personal assets of the partners. This would include their investments, cash, automobiles, etc. The landlord is not required to collect 20% of the debt from each of the partners. The landlord can go after the "deep pocket"—the partner with the most assets to satisfy the debt in full. That partner would be entitled to seek reimbursement for the amount he paid to the landlord from the other partners on a pro rata basis.

Example 2: A person operates a construction business. One of his employees operates a bulldozer that damages a set of power lines and causes a fire. The fire damages a nearby building. The damages exceed the amount of insurance coverage the business owner has in force. The owner may be sued for the amount of damages in excess of insurance coverage. His personal assets can be used to satisfy any judgment obtained against him with regard to the accident.

If the business is operated in the form of an FLP, any damages in excess of the insurance coverage can only be satisfied by the assets of the FLP. The personal assets of the owner would not be subject to risk.

The day-to-day operations of a corporation are controlled by officers elected by the board of directors. These officers most often include a president, treasurer, and secretary. A limited partnership's operations are controlled by the general partner. The general partner may or may not also be a limited partner. It is important that all of the operations of the FLP are conducted under the authority of the general partner. If a limited partner becomes involved in the daily activities of the FLP, the limited liability protection will be lost and the personal assets of the partner will be at risk. Additionally, like a shareholder of a corporation, if a limited partner personally guarantees an obligation of the FLP, he has placed his personal assets at risk.

Like corporations, if the FLP is not operated in accordance with applicable state statutes and observe the formalities required of a limited partnership, the FLP will be disregarded by the courts and the personal assets of the partners will be subject to risk. The formalities that need to be observed include the following:

- keeping the assets (particularly cash) separate from the partners personal assets;
- documenting the actions of the business in the name of the FLP (signing contracts, purchasing assets, etc.); and,
- keeping a separate record of the FLP's transactions.

Example: A limited partner is a medical doctor and a malpractice judgment is entered against him for $1 million. The plaintiff is now a judgment creditor who will try to collect the $1 million from the doctor. The judgment creditor would like to seize the partner's bank accounts and investments in order to collect the amount he is owed. However, the creditor discovers that the doctor no longer holds title to any of these assets. In fact, all of the assets have been transferred to the limited partnership.

Under the provisions of limited partnership law, a creditor of a partner cannot reach into the partnership and take specific partnership assets. The creditor has no rights to any property that is held by the partnership. Since the title to the assets is in the name of the partnership, it is the doctor who is liable for the debt, and partnership assets may not be taken to satisfy the judgment.

Because the judgment creditor cannot reach partnership assets, he can apply to the court for a charging order against the doctor's partnership interest. A *charging order* means that the general partner is directed to pay over to the judgment creditor any distributions from the partnership which would otherwise go to the partner until the judgment is paid in full. In other words, money which comes out of the partnership to the partner can be seized by the creditor until the amount of the judgment is satisfied. Cash distributions to the partner could therefore be taken by the creditor.

However, a charging order does not give the creditor the right to become a partner in the partnership and does not give him the right to interfere in the management or control of partnership affairs. He only receives the right to any actual distributions paid to the partner.

The PARTNERSHIP AGREEMENT often provides that if there is a charging order against a partner's interest, the partnership would not make any distributions to the partner. If the partnership does not make any distributions, the creditor receives no payments. The partnership retains all of its funds and continues to invest and reinvest its cash without making any distributions.

CONTINUOUS EXISTENCE

A limited partnership may have a specific period of existence or may remain in existence for the maximum number of years permitted by the state statute. The maximum number of years of a limited partnership's existence varies from state to state. Most partnerships are created to continue in existence for the maximum period of time allowed under state law. When a sole proprietor or an owner of a general partnership dies, the assets of the business may go to his heirs, but under state law the business ceases to exist. The business may be continued by the heirs of the business owner, but it will be viewed as a new business.

The death of one partner of an FLP may cause the business to be dissolved unless the partnership agreement provides to the contrary. Most **PARTNERSHIP AGREEMENTS** provide for the continuation of the partnership upon the death of a partner by permitting the partnership interest owned by the deceased partner to be owned by his or her heirs or by providing for the purchase of the partnership interest of the deceased partner by the partnership or the remaining partners.

Example: When a sole proprietor passes away, the assets used in the business will be given to his heirs or beneficiaries. If the heirs or beneficiaries want to continue the business, they must start over just as if they were creating a business from scratch. New tax numbers, licenses, and bank accounts must be established. Because the FLP is an entity with its own legal existence, the business can continue after the death of a partner without interruption and without the need to reestablish bank accounts, obtain new tax numbers, etc. (Most FLPs provide that upon the death of a partner, the interest of a deceased partner can be purchased by the remaining partners or the FLP itself.)

TRANSFERABILITY OF ASSETS

A sole proprietor owns the individual assets of the business. Therefore, if the assets are sold or transferred to heirs or beneficiaries, each separate asset must be transferred and rattled. Because the FLP is recognized as a separate legal entity, all of its assets and accounts are owned by the FLP. A partner owns an interest in the FLP—not its assets. Therefore, the assets of an FLP may be transferred by an assignment of the FLP assets. This is similar to the transfer of assets owned by a corporation.

Maintaining Control of the Business

One of the most popular reasons for creating an FLP is to allow a parent to share the profits of a business while maintaining control of the day-to-day operations of the business. Control can be maintained by the parents by retaining ownership of a majority of the limited partnership interests or by requiring a "super majority" vote of limited partners (for instance 66% or 75%). FLPs, like "ordinary" limited partnerships and corporations, can authorize limited partnership interests that have differing rights and privileges.

Example: Parents give their children limited partnership interests in the FLP. The parents want to retain control of the FLP. The limited partnership interests given to the children can be designed to have no voting rights while still being entitled to a share in the FLP profits.

As with any business entity, it is important that an FLP have separate bank accounts and records. Observing this formality will help to maintain the limited liability of the limited partners.

Income Tax Advantages

Some income tax advantages are available only to limited partnerships and certain types of corporations. The most important income tax advantage is that losses are fully deductible for an FLP. By contrast, an individual taxpayer must prove the business was engaged in for the purpose of making a profit before losses can be deducted. If the individual cannot prove that there was a profit motive, the Internal Revenue Service will consider the business to be a "hobby" and restrict the losses that can be taken on an individual's personal income tax return.

A limited partnership is a *pass-through entity*. A limited partnership is not a taxpaying entity, unlike a corporation or irrevocable trust. A limited partnership files an annual informational tax return setting forth its income and expenses but does not pay tax on its net income. Instead, each partner's proportionate share of income or loss is allocated to the individual partner. Each partner claims his share of deductions or reports his share of income on his own tax return. Use of a limited partnership avoids the potential for double taxation that exists if a C corporation is used. As a general rule, transfers of property into and out of an FLP will not ordinarily produce any tax consequences.

Ease of Estate Planning

Interests in an FLP can be distributed to beneficiaries under a will or trust rather easily. As noted above, the assets of a sole proprietorship must be individually transferred to heirs or beneficiaries. A limited partnership interest can be divided into separate shares to be distributed to various beneficiaries. Distributing the FLP interests through will or trust is another way FLPs can help provide for the family children.

Example: A father owns a 40% limited partnership interest in an FLP he created. He has four children, however, he wants to give a larger interest to his daughters than his sons. He then subdivides his interest into shares of 15%, 15%, 5% and 5%.

Estate and Gift Tax Savings

The value of a limited partnership interest in an FLP is subject to *discounting*. If a limited partner owns less than a *controlling interest* in an FLP, it is considered to be a *minority interest*. The value of the limited partnership interest is discounted because a willing buyer would not pay full value for the limited partnership interest to be involved in an entity in which the buyer is subject to the control of others. Additionally, a willing buyer would not pay full value for an interest in an FLP which is subject to restrictions on its transferability. (These discounts can range from 25% to 40%.)

Example: A father and mother each own a 49% limited partnership interest in the FLP they had created to own their family business. The FLP partnership agreement restricts ownership of a limited partnership to family members. The father wants to make a gift of 5% of his limited partnership interest to each of his two children. If the total value of the FLP is $100,000, then the father's interest (before discounts) is worth $49,000. Five percent of the father's interest is $2,450.00. However, the value can be reduced by 25% to 40% in recognition of the minority and lack of marketability discounts. For gift tax purposes, the value reported to the Internal Revenue Service would range from $1,470 to $1,835.

Use of an FLP and the valuation discounts associated with limited partnership interests permits transfers to other family members either during life or at death reduces the amount of gift and/or estate taxes that must be paid. This preserves the estate assets for the family. In effect, the FLP keeps more money "in the family" and available for a child's future.

SEPARATE CREDIT RATING

An FLP is a separate entity and can establish a separate credit rating. By obtaining loans or purchasing assets on credit and paying off the debt obligations, an FLP will have its own credit rating that is not connected with the credit rating of a partner. A partner may have a terrible credit rating, but the FLP may have an excellent credit rating.

DISADVANTAGES

As with any business entity, there are also disadvantages associated with an FLP. These include the following.

ADDITIONAL TAX RETURN

Although an FLP is not a separate taxpaying entity, it is required to file a separate tax return. The tax return is informational in that it reports the income, expenses, losses and credits of the FLP. These items are reported on the individual returns of the partners. The partnership tax return is more detailed than a *Schedule* C used to report the income of a sole proprietorship. The assistance of an accountant familiar with partnership taxation may be required. (Corporations are also required to file a separate tax return.)

ANNUAL REPORT

Most states require business entities such as corporations and limited partnerships to file an *annual report* with the secretary of state. This annual report often includes the name and address of the registered agent of the limited partnership, the name and address of the general partner, and the address of the principal place of business of the partnership. If the general partner is a corporation, the names and addresses of the officers may be required to be disclosed on the *annual report*.

SEPARATE RECORD KEEPING

An FLP must have its own records and keep written records of the management actions taken by the general partner on behalf of the limited partnership. An FLP must also maintain separate bank accounts, investment accounts, and the like.

CHECKING ACCOUNTS

Banks often refuse to cash checks payable to an FLP and often require that the funds be deposited into a business bank account. Withdrawals would have to be made from the business bank account, typically by checks. Most banks charge higher fees for business accounts than for individual accounts unless, minimum balances are maintained in the business accounts.

Start-Up Procedures 4

Naming Your Family Limited Partnership

Partnership law in all states requires that a name be given to a limited partnership. The first step in this process is to contact the secretary of state to determine if the proposed name for your FLP is available and is not being used by another corporation, limited liability company, or limited partnership in the state. In order to prevent public confusion, states require that business names not be alike.

Once you determine that the name is available, you may file a name reservation with the secretary of state. For a minimal fee, often ranging from $10–$50, the name for the FLP can be reserved for as many as 120 days. A name reservation prevents another business from using that name during the 120 days.

Assumed Names

You may decide to operate your business under a name other than the formal, legal name registered with the state. This *assumed* or *fictitious name* must also be registered with the state. Each state has procedures established to register an assumed or fictitious name.

An FLP can use a fictitious name for many reasons. Perhaps it operates more than one type of business. For instance, a family business that began as a plumbing business may have expanded into home remodeling.

the plumbing business may have been known as "Ron's Plumbing" for twenty-five years, but this name is not appropriate for a remodeling business. A separate FLP *does not need* to be formed to operate this business. Instead, an assumed name can be adopted and the business assets owned by the FLP but used in "Remodels by Ron."

FORBIDDEN NAMES

There are state and federal laws that control the use of certain words in the name of a limited partnership. If a forbidden word is used in the name of the FLP, the filing documents will be rejected and returned to you for correction. The prohibited words vary from state to state so it is important to check with your own state's rules. There are certain businesses that require special licensing or registration and cannot be used in the name of an FLP. Words that *typically* may not be used are:

Accounting	Cooperative
Bank	Disney
Banker	Insurance
Banking	Olympic
Credit Union	Trust Company
Trust	Federal
United States	Acceptance
Pharmacy	Medical
Indemnity	National
Guaranty	Thrift
Board of Trade	Chamber of Commerce
Certified Accountant	Architect
Engineering	Lawyer
Underwriter	Mortgage
Endowment	Savings
Loan	Doctor

CERTIFICATE OF PARTNERSHIP

An FLP is officially created when a **CERTIFICATE OF PARTNERSHIP** (in some states called the *Certificate of Existence*) is filed with the secretary of state with the appropriate filing fee. Once the **CERTIFICATE OF PARTNERSHIP** is reviewed and approved by the secretary of state, the state will issue a certificate officially recognizing the FLP. This certificate will become part of the official records of the FLP.

Almost all states have designed their own form of **CERTIFICATE OF LIMITED PARTNERSHIP**. These forms can be obtained by contacting the secretary of state. Many states have made partnership and corporate forms available on an official website. A list of these websites is contained in Appendix B.

You can use the form provided by the state or prepare your own form. The certificate included in this book is as simple as possible for this purpose. (see form 3, p.183.)

REQUIREMENTS

A **CERTIFICATE OF LIMITED PARTNERSHIP** will generally require only certain items to be recognized by the state. Additional information may be included in the certificate, but should more appropriately be included in the **LIMITED PARTNERSHIP AGREEMENT**.

At a minimum, the **CERTIFICATE OF LIMITED PARTNERSHIP** should include:

Name of Partnership. The name of the limited partnership must include one of the following four words:

Limited	Ltd.
Limited Partnership	L.P.

Use of one of these words puts the public on notice that the business with which they are dealing is a limited partnership. Not only does this help to preserve the limited liability protection of the partners, but also alerts persons dealing with the partnership to ensure that the representative of the FLP is authorized to act on behalf of the partnership.

Address of the FLP. The address of the principal office of the FLP, as well as the mailing address of the FLP, must be provided.

Term of FLP. The duration of the FLP must be stated in the certificate. The duration may be stated in terms of years or for as long as is permitted by state statute.

The name of the registered agent and the address of the registered office. Each FLP must have a registered agent and a registered office. The registered agent can be an individual or a corporation. If the registered agent is a corporation, the name of an individual officer, shareholder, or employee of the corporation must be listed in the certificate. The registered office can also be the business office of the FLP if the registered agent works in that office.

The purpose of the registered agent and registered office is to provide a person and physical location at which service of process can be made upon the FLP. There are some corporations that, for a fee, will serve as the registered office and registered agent for an FLP.

NOTE: *Post office boxes may be used as a mailing address but cannot be used as the address of the registered office.*

The name and address of the general partner of the partnership. The general partner may be any person, corporation, limited liability company, or other entity. If a corporation or other entity is the general partner, an officer of the corporation must be designated on the certificate and sign the certificate on behalf of the general partner. An FLP may have one or more general partners. Each general partner must be listed on the certificate and sign the certificate. (Many states require that the general partner be a resident of the state in which the FLP is organized.)

Purpose of partnership. The general activities or purpose of the FLP are set forth in the certificate.

Effective date. A specific effective date may be stated in the certificate, but is not required. If a delayed effective date is requested, state statutes should be checked to determine how long the effective date can be delayed. Some states do not permit an effective date more than thirty days after the certificate is filed. Unless otherwise provided, the certificate is effective upon filing and the FLP's official existence is recognized.

Signature. The CERTIFICATE OF LIMITED PARTNERSHIP must be signed by each general partner. Most states do not require that the signature of the general partner be notarized. If a corporation is a general partner, the name of the corporation must be included as well as the name and office held by the person who is signing the certificate and representing the corporation. If the name of the corporation and the office of the individual is not disclosed, the public may mistakenly believe that the individual himself is the general partner.

FILING

To be effective, the CERTIFICATE OF LIMITED PARTNERSHIP must be filed with the secretary of state. Most states require that the original certificate and one copy be filed. You should mail the certificates along with a TRANSMITTAL LETTER (form 1, p.179) and the filing fee. If you wish to receive a certified copy of the certificate, you may request it from the secretary of state for an additional fee. Some attorneys recommend sending an additional copy and request that the copy be returned to you with the date of receipt stamped on it. However, the date of receipt does not establish the existence of the FLP. A better alternative is to send the original documents and filing fee by certified mail return receipt requested. The return receipt will show that they received the documents.

After the certificate has been approved and filed, the secretary of state will send you a document that reflects the date on which the certificate was filed and the state charter number for the partnership. Most states return either the original certificate or a copy of the certificate that had been sent.

Processing and filing of the certificate by the secretary of state can vary from a few days to two weeks. December is typically a very busy month because many individuals want to form a limited partnership to be effective the following year. If there is a reason to have the certificate filed more quickly, the certificate may be sent by a courier or overnight delivery service.

There are companies in most states' capital cities that will accept delivery of the certificate and do a "walk through" (i.e. bring the certificate to the filing desk at the secretary of state's office) for a small fee. Whether sent by overnight mail or walked through, the certificate is filed the day it is received. Most states provide a "special handling" or "expedited handling" procedure by which the certificate will be processed before all other mail received that day. Usually there is an additional fee for this service.

Partnership Agreement

The **Partnership Agreement** is the heart of the limited partnership. The **Partnership Agreement** defines the rights and obligations between the general partner and the limited partners. The partnership agreement also defines the rights of each limited partner.

The Uniform Limited Partnership Act does not require a written partnership agreement. However, it is a very good idea to have a written agreement in place to specifically set forth the terms of the FLP and the rights, duties and obligations of the partners. (Chapter 5 is devoted to the partnership agreement and covers in detail the many provisions of a partnership agreement.)

Tax Forms

Form SS-4 (Employer Identification Number)

Every business must obtain a *taxpayer identification number*—the business' equivalent of a social security number. This number is required to open bank accounts in the name of the business. To obtain a taxpayer identification number, a partnership must file **IRS Form SS-4.** (see form 11, p.203.) **IRS Form SS-4** is filed either by mail or by fax with the Internal Revenue Service. It generally takes two to three weeks to receive a response from the IRS. At some times of the year, the IRS is overloaded with requests and it may take as long as four to five weeks. The instructions to **IRS Form SS-4** that are included with **IRS Form SS-4** identifies the IRS Service Center that handles filings for the state where your FLP is formed.

The IRS has provided telephone numbers assigned to various regions of the country that can be called to obtain the employer identification number quickly. You must have completed **IRS Form SS-4** so that you can give the IRS agent the information needed to receive the number. The IRS agent will assign a taxpayer identification number to your FLP.

Once the FLP has been assigned a taxpayer identification number, the IRS will send you information regarding partnership tax forms and information from the IRS on the new business. Among the information is a *Circular E* that sets forth the requirements for withholding taxes from wages for any employee of the partnership, deposit coupons for payroll taxes, and IRS Form 941 quarterly return for employment tax withholding.

Bank Accounts

As with any form of business, it is important for an FLP to have a bank account and that all checks payable to the FLP be deposited into the FLP bank account (most banks will not cash checks that are payable to the FLP). It is also important to make these deposits as a means of recording the income of the FLP. An FLP must maintain a bank account to pay expenses and make distributions to partners as authorized by the general partner.

Only the general partner will have signature authority on the bank account for the FLP. If a limited partner is given signature authority on the bank account, the limited liability protection usually accorded to a limited partner may be lost. Banks will require a copy of the documents received from the state showing that the FLP is legally recognized by the state. The bank will also require the FLP's taxpayer identification number.

Licensing

Many states require permits and licenses for certain types of businesses. These include real estate brokers, hairdressers, barbers, pharmacies, private investigators, restaurants, notaries, educational institutions, food services, employment agencies, businesses serving or selling alcohol or tobacco products, aviation, drug manufacturing, and the like. Federal agencies also regulate many businesses and it will be necessary to check with them to determine what regulations are applicable to your business. If your FLP conducts one of these types of businesses, you may have to apply for a permit or license.

Payroll Taxes

If you are going to hire employees for your business, you will be required to file state and federal tax reports. Additionally, you will be subject to withholding local, state, and federal taxes and be required to pay social security tax, Medicare tax, and unemployment insurance or workers' compensation.

Record Keeping

It is important that separate books and records for the FLP are maintained to track expenses and income. Because the FLP is a separate legal entity under the law, it must maintain an "identity" separate from its owners—the general and limited partners. It is not necessary to keep an elaborate set of books for the FLP. A simple accounting system that clearly shows what the FLP takes in and distributes is all that is required. (Very simple accounting or bookkeeping computer programs, such as Quickbooks or Peachtree Accounting can be purchased at local retail stores.)

Annual Report

Most states require business entities to file an annual report with the secretary of state or the state treasurer. Generally, a small fee must be paid when this report is filed. The purpose of the annual report is to keep the state informed of the current information pertaining to the FLP. This includes the name and address of the registered agent, the address of the principal office, and the name and address of the general partner.

5 The Family Limited Partnership Agreement

There is no requirement that an FLP adopt a "written" partnership agreement. However, if there is no written partnership agreement, the state's limited partnership statutes will apply and control all aspects of the operation of the FLP. This includes the rights of partners, allocation of income and expenses among the partners, voting rights of the partners and dissolution of the FLP. It is best to create a partnership agreement that reduces to writing the agreement of the partners as to the terms and conditions of the FLP.

Key Provisions

The *family limited partnership agreement* may be as simple or complex as the partners desire. The following are key provisions to include in the **Partnership Agreement**:

- name of the FLP;
- address of the FLP;
- state of formation;
- name and address of the general partner(s);
- name and address of each limited partner;

- purpose of the FLP and the nature of its business;
- effective date of the FLP;
- term or duration of the FLP;
- requirements to keep books and financial records;
- rights of partners to inspect books and financial records;
- contributions of each partner and conditions and dates for the return of capital to partners;
- duties and powers of general partner;
- procedures and power to replace general partner;
- conditions allowing partners to terminate or assign their interests;
- conditions for dissolving the FLP;
- voting rights of limited partners;
- voting rights of general partner;
- statement of limited liability for the limited partners;
- methods for allocating profits and losses among partners;
- right of general partner to withhold distributions;
- conditions and procedures for amending partnership agreement;
- obligations of limited partners to make additional contributions or loans to the FLP;
- method of accounting for and apportioning taxes among partners;
- accounting/fiscal year of FLP (generally this must be January 1 through December 31);
- designation of a tax matters partner for the FLP;
- provision for resolution of disputes between partners through mediation or arbitration;

- requirement for meetings of partners; and,
- signatures of partners.

Partners' Signatures

Of course, the most important part of the partnership agreement is the signatures of the general and limited partners. Without the date and partners' signatures, the partnership agreement is ineffective. It is equally important that as new partners are admitted to the FLP, either by purchasing an interest from the partnership or from another partner, or by obtaining the interest by gift or inheritance, the new partners sign the partnership agreement. If the new partner does not sign the partnership agreement, he or she will not be bound by its terms and, therefore, not be entitled to receive the benefits of the FLP interest he now owns.

Business Purpose

In recent years, the Internal Revenue Service has checked the validity of an FLP based on the argument that the partnership had no valid business purpose. Therefore, it is very important to set forth a business purpose for the FLP. Appendix C lists business purposes that have been recognized by the IRS as valid.

6 Taxation of the Family Limited Partnership

Partnerships are not taxpayers; however, the partnership must determine its taxable income. Partnership income is determined in the same manner as individuals, except deductions are not allowed for personal exemptions, foreign taxes, net operating loss carrybacks and carryforwards, charitable contributions, itemized deductions, capital loss carryovers, or depletion deductions.

The partnership does not pay income tax and is referred to as a pass-through entity. The partners pay the taxes on partnership income, even if the income is not actually distributed to the partners. This holds true even if the partners cannot withdraw their shares, but must retain them in the partnership as capital.

The PARTNERSHIP AGREEMENT largely controls the allocation of taxable income or losses, or any other income item, gain, loss, deduction or credit. Tax allocations are usually based on the ratio to set a partner's share of profits or losses from business operations, and with gains, etc., allocated in a similar manner.

IRS Form 1065—United States Partnership Income Tax Return

FLPs are not subject to income tax. The income, losses, expenses, and other deductions will be reported on the individual income tax return (**IRS Form 1040**) of the partners. However, the FLP is required to file a tax return that is essentially an information return. **IRS Form 1065** reflects all of the items of income, expense, gain, loss, and deduction attributed to the FLP. Each partner is given a **Schedule K-1** that reflects the partners proportionate share of these items. The items shown on **Schedule K-1** are reported on the partner's **IRS Form 1040**.

Partnership returns must be filed the first year that the FLP has income and deductions. Thereafter, the IRS will expect an **IRS Form 1065** annually, even if the FLP has no reportable income. The general partner is required to sign the return on behalf of the FLP.

Most partnerships operate on a calendar year, rather than a fiscal year. The taxable year of the FLP must be the same as the taxable year of one or more partners whose aggregate interest in the FLP profits and capital exceeds 50%. Calendar year partnerships must file **IRS Form 1065** before or on April 15 after the partnership's taxable year. If the FLP needs additional time to file **IRS Form 1065**, it may obtain an automatic extension for three months.

Calculating Taxable Income

In calculating taxable income from a partnership, there are two methods of accounting that can be used. The *cash method* reports income from cash or property when actually received or expended and not when earned or accrued. The *accrual method* has income derived when the partnership receives the right to receive the cash or property, and a liability when it is actually incurred rather than when paid.

When a partner contributes cash, property, or services to the partnership in exchange for an FLP interest, the partner is credited with the *fair market value* of the property at the time of the contribution. This establishes the partner's *initial tax basis* in the FLP. The partners are only changing the form of their assets—from cash or property to an FLP interest. Therefore, neither gain nor loss is realized upon contribution. Transferring assets to an FLP does not create a taxable event for the contributing partners, regardless of whether the FLP is newly formed or has been in existence for a long time.

If a partner is given an interest in an FLP, the new partner is credited with the fair market value of the partnership interest at the time of the gift. This establishes the partner's initial tax basis in the FLP.

When services are transferred to a partnership in exchange for a partnership interest, a different rule applies. Services rendered are not "property." Therefore, the partner providing the services is considered to be receiving compensation that is characterized as ordinary income. The compensation received from the partnership is equal to the capital interest received and is considered taxable income in the year the services are provided.

PROFIT'S INTEREST

If a *profit's interest* (a share of earnings and profits) is received, then another rule applies. When services are traded for a profits interest, the contribution of services is taxable only upon receiving the profits because the fair market value of future profits cannot be determined earlier.

Partnership income is decreased by the amount of such distributions to the partners (as for salaries or expenses). It is also decreased by partnership losses, plus the partner's share of nondeductible expenses that cannot be charged to the partner's capital account.

Purchasing an existing FLP interest from another partner rather than from the FLP does not fall within this rule. These purchases are considered the same as purchasing other property. The initial basis equals the cost of the acquired interest that is equal to what he pays for the interest plus the selling partner's share of any FLP debts assumed by the purchasing partner.

Calculating Tax from Dissolution of FLP

To calculate the tax consequences from the sale, liquidation, or dissolution of the FLP interest, the tax value of the interest must be determined. The partner's tax basis also serves as the ceiling on the amount of loss that a partner may deduct from his taxable income. The value of an FLP interest is easily determined when cash is contributed in exchange for the interest. If property is contributed to the FLP, the value of the partnership interest is the adjusted basis of the property when it is contributed. If the property is subject to debts, mortgages, or other encumbrances, the partner's basis is reduced by the indebtedness assumed by the FLP.

At the end of the partnership's taxable year, the partner's interest is adjusted upward or downward. Distributions to partners are taxed only when the cash received exceeds the partner's adjusted basis in his partnership interest. A partner may only deduct losses on his personal income tax return to the extent the losses do not exceed the partner's basis in the partnership at the end of the partnership's taxable year.

State Sales Tax

If you will be selling or renting goods or services at retail, you must collect state sales and use tax. Some services such as doctors' and lawyers' fees are not taxed, but most others are. If you have any doubt, check with the comptroller or treasurer of the state. You must obtain a tax number, which requires you to fill out a simple questionnaire. To obtain this form, you can call the comptroller or treasurer (your local office should be listed in the beginning of your telephone book under State Government Offices). After you obtain your tax number, you will be required to collect sales tax on all purchases. Tax returns must be filed quarterly, but in many states, if your taxes are low after a year, you may be allowed to file the return annually.

7 Transferring Assets to the Family Limited Partnership

Once the FLP has been established, assets must be transferred to it in order to begin doing business. The partnership uses the assets contributed to it by its partners, whether general or limited, to begin doing business. It is very important to determine which assets will be transferred to the partnership and which assets will remain owned by the partners individually.

Dangerous Assets

There are certain assets that an FLP should not own for various tax and legal reasons. It is important to check with your accountant and lawyer to determine which assets should be transferred to the FLP. Typically, assets transferred to the FLP should have a business or investment purpose. There are certain assets that have tax advantages associated with them and, if contributed to an FLP, they would lose these tax advantages. Among the assets that *should not be transferred* to the FLP are the following:

- your personal residence;
- S corporation stock;
- IRAs;
- SEP-IRAs;

- other qualified or tax-deferred retirement plans; and,
- annuities.

Your *personal residence* should not be transferred to the FLP because it enjoys protection from creditor's under your state's homestead laws. Also, the income tax deduction for home-mortgage interest is permitted only for a "qualified residence," defined under the tax code as an individual's principal residence. If the FLP owns the principal residence, this tax deduction is lost. Also, the deductibility of property taxes may be more beneficial if taken by an individual directly on his income tax return rather than by the FLP. Finally, any personal residence owned by an FLP no longer qualifies for the one-time capital gain exclusion available to individual taxpayers.

By law, *S corporation stock* cannot be owned by a limited partnership. However, stock in a C corporation or limited liability company can be owned by a limited partnership.

Pensions and *retirement plans* must be kept in separate accounts and, by operation of federal law, cannot be titled in the name of a limited partnership.

Finally, while *annuities* can legally be transferred to a limited partnership, the tax deferral benefits of the annuity may be lost, significantly reducing the benefit of transferring the annuities to the limited partnership.

Safe Assets

Keep in mind that one of the primary advantages of an FLP is to protect assets from the claims of creditors. The following is a representative list of assets that *can be transferred* to an FLP:

- vacation home;
- rental/commercial property;
- vacant or farm land;

- time-share condominiums;
- automobiles, boats, airplanes;
- life insurance policies;
- money market funds;
- mutual funds;
- stocks and bonds;
- business inventory, equipment and supplies;
- patents, trademarks, copyrights and other proprietary rights;
- accounts receivable;
- jewelry, antiques, artwork, and other tangible property;
- mortgages, notes receivable, promissory notes;
- contract rights and interests; and,
- C corporation stock in closely-held corporations.

When selecting assets that will be transferred to the FLP, you must keep in mind the business purpose of the FLP. If the FLP purpose is to manufacture widgets, vacant real estate or farm land should not be transferred to the FLP. An FLP should not own assets that are unrelated to its business purpose. If the business purpose of the FLP is very broad, such as the management of investment assets, most of the assets listed above can be transferred to the FLP.

In determining which assets to transfer to the FLP, you should consider whether the transfer of the asset can be easily accomplished. Is the asset jointly owned and require the approval of a joint owner? Will the transfer disrupt previously established arrangements or relationships? Will outside partners own interests in the FLP? If so, are you willing to give up sole control and ownership of the asset by transferring it to the FLP?

How to Transfer Assets

After you have identified which assets you will transfer to the FLP, titles to those assets must be legally transferred to the partnership. These transfers are accomplished in the same manner as if the assets were transferred to another individual. The following procedures are used to transfer assets to the FLP:

- ***Real estate—by deed***
  If real estate that is subject to a mortgage is being transferred, you must obtain the permission of the mortgage holder to transfer title. Recording costs must be considered because they can be expensive. A quitclaim deed is included in the forms to be used for this purpose. Determine whether the transfer of real estate results in a revaluation of the property for tax purposes. Question whether zoning or easement rights may be lost if the property is transferred.

- ***Personal property—by bill of sale or general assignment***
  If trucks, boats or automobiles are transferred to the partnership, you will be required to obtain a new registration and new insurance. You should also check to see if there will be a sales tax that must be paid upon the transfer. A general assignment form is included in the forms to be used for this purpose.

- ***Stocks, bonds, mutual funds and other investments—by assignment or endorsement and delivery of the ownership certificate.***
  To transfer these assets, you can call your broker or the transfer agent that handles your particular assets. Generally, they will be able to prepare all of the paperwork necessary for the transfer. You should keep in mind that certain assets, such as certificates of deposits, may be subject to a penalty if title is transferred prior to maturity. You should check with your bank or financial institution as to whether this is the case prior to transferring title. A

general assignment form is included in the forms to be used for the transfer of assets other than those which will require paperwork provided by your broker or the transfer agent.

- ***Notes and mortgages—by endorsement***
  Any asset that is transferred to the FLP that is subject to an insurance policy must have that insurance policy reissued in the name of the FLP. Because the FLP now owns the asset, any proceeds from the insurance must be payable to the FLP.

  NOTE: *The policy may require higher premiums or you may be required to pay a penalty for cancelling your current policy. Be certain to check with your insurance agent before transferring these assets.*

8 Amending an FLP Agreement

Partnership Agreement

Rarely will a **Partnership Agreement** *need* to be amended. However, a **Partnership Agreement** *may* be amended for the following reasons:

- to change the name of your FLP;
- to change the management rights of the general partner;
- to add a special clause such as a higher than majority voting requirement; or,
- to create another class of partnership interests.

The amendment must be signed by all of the partners of the FLP. The amendment to **Partnership Agreement** need not be filed with the secretary of state or any other governmental entity.

Registered Agent or Registered Office

If the registered agent or registered office of an FLP is changed, the change must be reported to the secretary of state along with a filing fee. (see form 9, p.199.) Some states impose a penalty if the change of registered agent or registered office is not reported to the secretary of state.

9 Dissolution of a Family Limited Partnership

A business entity, whether a corporation, general or limited partnership, or limited liability company can be dissolved in either of two ways—voluntarily or involuntarily.

Voluntary Dissolution

An FLP may be *voluntarily dissolved* in the following ways:

- by the agreement of the partners;
- the withdrawal of a partner; or,
- by expiration of the period for existence as set forth in the **Partnership Agreement**.

Most states provide that a FLP may continue in existence for a limited number of years from the date of its formation. This may vary from thirty to fifty years. The partnership agreement may also provide that the partnership will expire upon the happening of one or more events. These events of expiration must be set forth in the **Certificate of Limited Partnership** that is filed with the secretary of state.

Many states permit a partnership to continue existing even if a partner wants to withdraw. States do this by allowing the remaining partners or the partnership itself to purchase the interest of the withdrawing partner. In most cases, prior notice of the withdrawal must be given to the partners. Additionally, many states now permit an FLP to continue if the partner withdraws and if the remaining partners agree to continue the partnership. The partnership agreement should contain provisions that address either of these situations.

Involuntary Dissolution

An FLP may be forced into *involuntary dissolution* by a court or by operation of the statutes for:

- failure to pay taxes (whether income, franchise, sales, etc.);
- failure to maintain a registered agent or registered office for the partnership;
- misconduct of the partnership including failure to return a partnership contribution to a partner;
- merger of the partnership into another entity;
- failure to file required reports and pay fees; and/or,
- engaging in business activities that limited partnerships are prohibited from conducting under state law.

Valuation of FLP Interest

When a partner withdraws from an FLP, the value of the partner's interest must be determined and the method by which the partner will receive payment for his interest must be established. The value of an FLP interest may be determined in one of several methods:

- ***Buyout Clause.*** The partnership agreement may require that a professional appraiser be hired to value the withdrawing partner's interest. Alternatively, the partnership agreement may provide that the value of the FLP interest be arbitrated with the withdrawing partner with the remaining partners obtaining separate appraisals.

- ***Asset Value Method.*** The value of the FLP interest is determined by calculating the net worth of the FLP subtracting the liabilities from the assets. The withdrawing partner receives his proportionate share of the new worth.

- ***Fixed Method.*** All partners may periodically agree to pay a fixed price to a withdrawing partner. This fixed price is determined at fixed intervals during the existence of the FLP.

- ***Original Contribution Method.*** Regardless of when the partner withdraws from the FLP, he is only entitled to receive the value of his original contribution to the FLP. If the FLP interest was gifted to the partner, the partner is only entitled to receive the value of the interest at the time of the gift.

After the method of valuation has been determined, the method of payment must also be determined. You can provide that periodic payments be made or that the payment be made in a single lump sum. If the partnership agreement does not provide a method of payment, the *Uniform Limited Partnership Act* (see Appendix D) will act as the default rule and will require a lump sum payment.

Dissolution Procedure

Whether the FLP is being dissolved involuntarily or voluntarily, the dissolution procedures remains the same.

1. The assets of the partnership must be distributed to the partners. Generally, the distribution will be done in accordance with the partner's ownership interest in the FLP.

2. Clients and creditors must be notified of the dissolution of the FLP. This should be done by written notification of the termination.
3. Federal and state tax authorities and agencies must be notified of the dissolution of the FLP. This includes federal, state and local income tax agencies, employment agencies, and regulatory agencies.
4. Debts of the FLP must be paid or provision must be made for payment.
5. A final accounting should be prepared and provided to the partners.

Dissolution Documents

Each state requires that the FLP file certain documents with the secretary of state upon dissolution. This is true whether the dissolution is voluntary or involuntary. Typically, the documents include *Articles of Dissolution, Termination or Cancellation* and *Notice of Intent to Dissolve,* which is a public notice that is sent to creditors and is published in a local newspaper. The Notice of Intent to Dissolve is sent to creditors to put the creditors on notice of a cut-off date for filing a claim against the partnership and gives the creditor notice that the FLP will no longer be conducting business.

These forms are different from state to state, as are the states' individual form usage and filing requirements. You should contact your secretary of state for forms and requirements.

Conclusion 10

Creating a family limited partnership is a great way to protect your current assets by avoiding personal liability, and at the same time providing for the future needs of family members, such as your children. As you can see, it is an effective and relatively easy method of preserving and safeguarding your current business interests as well as your children's financial future. I hope you have found this book helpful.

Good luck on your new family business!

Glossary

A

accrual method. A financial record-keeping system that credits income when earned or due and expenses when incurred, regardless of actual cash receipts or disbursements.

adjusted basis. Original cost or value adjusted by additions and depreciation.

assets. Anything owned with monetary value. This includes both real and personal property.

asset protection. A form of financial self-defense that places assets beyond the reach of creditors.

assumed name. *See* business name.

B

business name. Trade name or commercial name used to identify a specific business.

C

calendar year. The accounting year beginning January 1 and ending on December 31.

capital. *See* assets.

cash method. A financial record-keeping system relying on actual cash receipts or actual cash disbursements at the time of receipt or disbursement.

certificate of limited partnership. Document filed with a governmental agency to record the existence of the partnership for official purposes.

charging order. A statutorily created means for a creditor of a judgment debtor who is a partner of others to reach the debtor's beneficial interest in the partnership, without risking dissolution of the partnership.

continuous existence. A period of existence of an entity that is not limited by time or statute.

corporation. A business formed and authorized by law to act as a single entity, although it may be owned by one or more persons. It is legally endowed with rights and responsibilities and has a life of its own independent of the owners and operators. The owners are not personally liable for debts or obligations of the corporation.

D

deceptively similar. A name so similar to another name that the two may become confused to the public.

dissolution. Formal statutory liquidation, termination and winding up of a business entity.

distribution. Payment of cash or property to a member, shareholder or partner in accordance with his or her percentage of ownership in the entity.

double taxation. This occurs when a corporation pays tax on its profits and its shareholders pay income tax on dividend or distributive income.

E

ease of transferability. The ability to transfer ownership interests without the consent or approval of other owners, shareholders, or partners.

employer identification number. A number issued by the Internal Revenue Service to identify a business for tax purposes.

F

family limited partnership. Type of partnership that is comprised of lineal family members, usually with a parent as a general partner (or in control of the general partner) and children as limited partners.

fiscal year. A 12-month period used by a business as its fiscal accounting period.

G

general partner. The partner (a person or entity) who accepts personal liability and is responsible for the daily management of a partnership.

general partnership. The basic type of partnership where all partners share equal contributions, distributions, and liability, as well as equal responsibility in all partnership affairs.

I

insolvency. Business liabilities in excess of business assets.

J

judgment creditor. A creditor who has obtained a court-ordered judgment against a debtor.

L

liability. Being responsible for possible or actual loss, penalty, expense, or burden; being bound or obligated by law or justice to do, pay, or make good something.

limited liability. With regard to corporations or limited liability companies, the owners' freedom from being personally liable for the debts and obligations of the business. Generally, creditors of the business cannot reach the personal assets of the owners, members or shareholders.

limited liability company. A form of business entity created by statute that is similar to a corporation with regard to limited liability but is treated like a partnership for tax purposes

limited partner. A partner who contributes capital or property to the partnership in exchange for an interest in the profits of the partnership. The partner enjoys limited liability to the extent of his or her investment in the partnership. The partner may not participate in the management of the partnership affairs.

limited partnership. A type of partnership where there is at least one general partner (a person or entity) who has complete liability and control of the business and in which there are one or more limited partners who can invest assets with limited liability, with no control in the affairs of the business.

M

mediation. The action of a disinterested third party to reconcile or settle any differences between parties who have disagreements. The result of mediation is not legally binding upon the parties.

P

partnership. A legal entity formed when two or more individuals or entities agree to carry on a business together.

partnership agreement. A document that sets forth the rights, duties, and obligations of the partners of a limited partnership. The document also sets forth the terms and conditions of the liquidation of the partnership and the admission of new partners.

pass-through entity. An entity that is not taxed on its profits. Its profits are distributed directly to its owners who report such profits as income on their personal income tax returns.

personal liability. The personal assets (such as home, automobile, personal investments, etc.) of an individual are subject to the claims of creditors of a business.

R

registered agent. The person designated to receive legal papers that are to be served on the business entity.

S

securities. Stocks, bonds, notes, and other documents that represent a share in a company or a debt owed by a company or governmental entity.

shareholder. *See* stockholder.

silent partner. A limited partner whose name does not appear in the name of the business and takes no active role in the operations of the business, but has an interest in the profits of the business.

sole proprietorship. A business owned by an individual who is solely responsible for all aspects of the business. The business and its owner are considered to be the same entity.

stockholder. The owner of one or more shares of stock of a corporation. A stockholder may also be called a shareholder.

T

tax basis. The value assigned to an asset for the purpose of determining gain or loss for income tax purposes.

U

uniform limited partnership act. Regulations for limited partnerships adopted by most of the 50 states and the District of Columbia with minor modifications.

Appendix A
Checklist for Forming a Family Limited Partnership

As you create your Family Limited Partnership, use this checklist to ensure that you have completed every essential step in the process. Once every task is checked off, you know you have successfully formed a Family Limited Partnership, and you are ready to start running your new business.

Family Limited Partnership Start-Up Checklist

- ❒ Review the state statutes relating to the formation and governance of limited partnerships.
- ❒ Contact the secretary of state to determine the filing fee for a limited partnership.
- ❒ Select a name for the limited partnership.
- ❒ If necessary, reserve the name for the limited partnership with the secretary of state until the official partnership documents are prepared and filed with the state.
- ❒ If a corporation, limited liability company, or trust will serve as general partner of the limited partnership, prepare all of the documents necessary to create the general partner.
- ❒ Identify the registered agent and registered office for the limited partnership.
- ❒ Identify the annual fees that may be charged for the limited partnership. This includes a filing fee for an annual report or an annual franchise tax.
- ❒ Identify any state or local income taxes that will be charged to the limited partnership and how they will be determined.
- ❒ Meet with an accountant to discuss capitalization and tax planning.
- ❒ If necessary, meet with a securities lawyer regarding stock sales.
- ❒ Prepare the **Certificate of Limited Partnership**. (see form __, p.___.)
- ❒ Prepare the **Limited Partnership Agreement**. (see form ___, p.___.)
- ❒ File **Certificate of Limited Partnership** with your secretary of state.
- ❒ File **Application for Employer Identification Number (IRS Form SS-4)** with the Internal Revenue Service to obtain a federal taxpayer identification number. (see form __, p.___.)
- ❒ Issue partnership interests.
  - Make certain that consideration is paid for the partnership interests
  - Complete bill of sale, assignments, or other documents required to transfer assets to the limited partnership.
- ❒ File necessary forms with state to obtain state income and/or sales tax identification number.
- ❒ Open a bank account.
- ❒ Obtain city or county licenses, if needed.
- ❒ Obtain ring binder for organizational documents.

Appendix B
State-By-State Limited Partnership Requirements

Organized by state, this appendix is a quick reference guide to the basic requirements each particular state has on forming a family limited partnership. It includes your state's name requirements, record-keeping rules, forms you must complete and various fees.

Also, a very good general website is **www.Megalaw.com**. This website provides direct links to various websites for each state. These links include state statutes, cases, codes and regulations, state courts, legal forms, legislation, and state bar and legal associations.

ALABAMA

Alabama Secretary of State Corporation Division
P.O. Box 5616
Montgomery, AL 36103
334-242-5324
www.sos.state.al.us

Name Requirements

Must include "limited" or "Ltd." The name may not include "bank," "banking," "banker," "trust," "insurance," "corporation," "incorporated," or any abbreviation of these words. The name may not include the name of a limited partner unless it is also the name of a general partner or the business of the limited partnership has used that name before admission of that limited partner.

Record Keeping Office Maintained Within State

Must continuously maintain an office in state where required records are kept, which need not be the place of the partnership's business.

Required Forms

Certificate of Limited Partnership. One original and one copy to the Probate Judge in the county where the registered office is located.

Report of Limited Partnership. Submit to secretary of state within thirty days of filing the Certificate of Limited Partnership.

Combined Initial Business Privilege Tax Return, Corporate Shares Tax Return, Annual Report. Submit to the Department of Revenue within thirty days after the date of incorporation.

Minimum Fees

State filing fee: $5

County fees: Vary. Montgomery County: $1, plus $2.50 per page.

ALASKA

Division of Banking, Securities and Corporations
Department of Commerce and Economic Development
P.O. Box 110808
Juneau, AK 99811
907-465-2530
www.dced.state.ak.us/

Name Requirements

Must include the words "limited partnership" without abbreviation. The name may not include the name of a limited partner unless it is also the name of a general partner or the corporate name of a corporate general partner, or the business of the limited partnership has used that name before admission of the limited partner.

Record Keeping Office Maintained Within State

Must continuously maintain an office in state where required records are kept, which need not be a place of the partnership's business.

Required Forms

Certificate of Limited Partnership. Submit one original and one copy to the Department of Commerce and Economic Development.

Minimum Fees

$150.

ARIZONA

Arizona Corporation Commission
Corporations Division
1300 W. Washington, 1st Floor
Phoenix, AZ 85007
602-542-3135
www.cc.state.az.us

NAME REQUIREMENTS

Must include the words "limited partnership" without abbreviation. The name may not include the name of a limited partner unless it is also the name of a general partner or the business of the limited partnership has used that name before admission of the limited partner.

RECORD KEEPING OFFICE MAINTAINED WITHIN STATE

Must continuously maintain office in state where required records are kept, which need not be a place of the partnership's business.

REQUIRED FORMS

Certificate of Limited Partnership. Submit two copies to the Arizona Corporation Commission.

MINIMUM FEES

$10, plus $3 per page.

ARKANSAS

Secretary of State
Corporations Division
State Capitol
Little Rock, AR 72201
501-682-3409
www.sosweb.state.ar.us

NAME REQUIREMENTS

Must include the words "limited partnership" without abbreviation. The name may not include the name of a limited partner unless it is also the name of a general partner or the corporate name of a corporate general partner or the business of the limited partnership has used that name before admission of the limited partner.

RECORD KEEPING OFFICE MAINTAINED WITHIN STATE

Must continuously maintain an office in state where required records are kept, which need not be a place of the partnership's business.

REQUIRED FORMS

Certificate of Limited Partnership and the Articles of Partnership. Submit two copies of each to the secretary of state.

MINIMUM FEES

$50.

CALIFORNIA

California Secretary of State
Limited Partnership Unit
P.O. Box 944225
Sacramento, CA 94244-2250
916-653-3365
www.ss.ca.gov/business/business.htm

NAME REQUIREMENTS

Must include the words "limited" or "Ltd." The name may include a limited partner's name. The name may not include the words "bank," "insurance," "trust," "trustee," "incorporated," "corporation," or an abbreviation of these words.

RECORD KEEPING OFFICE MAINTAINED WITHIN STATE

Must maintain an office in state where required records are kept.

REQUIRED FORMS

Certificate of Limited Partnership. Submit one original and one copy to the secretary of state.

MINIMUM FEES

$70, plus $15 counter fee if hand delivered.

COLORADO

Colorado Secretary of State
Business Division
1560 Broadway, Suite 200
Denver, CO 80202-5169
303-894-2200
www.sos.state.co.us/pubs/business/main.htm

Name Requirements

Must include the words "limited partnership," "limited," "company," "L.P.," "Ltd.," or "Co." The name may not include the name of a limited partner unless it is also the name of a general partner or the corporate name of a corporate general partner or the business of the limited partnership has used that name before admission of the limited partner.

Record Keeping Office Maintained Within State

Must continuously maintain a registered office in state where required records are kept, which need not be a place of the partnership's business.

Required Forms

Certificate of Limited Partnership. Submit two copies to the secretary of state.

Minimum Fees

$50.

CONNECTICUT

Secretary of the State
30 Trinity Street
Hartford, CT 06106
860-509-6079
www.sots.state.ct.us/Business/BusinessMain.html

Name Requirements

Must include the words "limited partnership" without abbreviation. The name may not include the name of a limited partner unless it is also the name of a general partner or the business of the limited partnership has used that name before admission of the limited partner.

Record Keeping Office Maintained Within State

Must continuously maintain an office in state where required records are kept.

Required Forms

Certificate of Limited Partnership. Submit one copy to secretary of state.

Minimum Fees

$60.

DELAWARE

Division of Corporations
John G. Townsend Building
401 Federal Street - Suite #4
Dover, DE 19901
302-739-3073
www.state.de.us/corp.htm

Name Requirements

Must include the words "limited partnership" or the abbreviation "L.P." The name may include these words: "company," "club," "association," "foundation," "fund," "institute," "society," "union," "syndicate," "limited," "trust," or abbreviations of these words.

Record Keeping Office Maintained Within State

No record keeping requirements for a limited partnership.

Required Forms

Certificate of Limited Partnership. Submit one original to the Division of Corporations.

Minimum Fees

$200.

DISTRICT OF COLUMBIA

Corporations Division
941 North Capitol Street NE,
Washington DC 20002
202-442-4432
dcra.dc.gov/information/build_pla/business_services/corporations_division.shtm

Name Requirements

Must include the words "limited partnership" or "L.P." The name may not include the name of a limited partner unless it is also the name of a general partner or the business of the limited partnership has used that name before admission of the limited partner.

Record Keeping Office Maintained Within State

Must continuously maintain office in the District of Columbia where required records are kept, which need not be a place of the partnership's business.

Required Forms

Certificate of Limited Partnership and consent of Registered Agent. Submit two copies to the Department of Consumer and Regulatory Affairs.

FLORIDA

Department of State
Division of Corporations
Corporate Filings
P.O. Box 6327
Tallahassee, FL 32314
General Inquiries: 850-488-9000
Limited Partnership Filings: 850-245-6051
ccfcorp.dos.state.fl.us/

Name Requirements

Must include "limited" or "Ltd." The name may not include the name of a limited partner unless it is also the name of a general partner or the business of the limited partnership has used that name before admission of the limited partner.

Record Keeping Office Maintained Within State

Must continuously maintain an office in state where required records are kept, which need not be the place of the partnership's business.

Required Forms

Certificate of Limited Partnership and the Affidavit of Capital Contributions. Submit one original and one copy to the Department of State.

Minimum Fees

Based on total amount contributed and anticipated by the limited partners, as shown: $7 per $1000 contribution-minimum fee, $52.50 plus $35 for designation of agent.

GEORGIA

Corporations Division
James H. Floyd Veterans Memorial Building
315 West Tower
#2 Martin Luther King, Jr. Drive
Atlanta, GA 30334-1530.
404-656-2817
www.sos.state.ga.us/corporations/
or
www.GeorgiaCorporations.org

Name Requirements

Must include the words "limited partnership" or "L.P." If the name on the certificate does not include one of these, the secretary of state will add the ending "L.P."

Record Keeping Office Maintained Within State

Must continuously maintain a registered office in state where required records are kept.

Required Forms

Certificate of Limited Partnership and Transmittal Information Form. Submit one original and one copy to the Corporations Division.

Minimum Fees

$60.

HAWAII

Department of Commerce and Consumer Affairs
Business Registration Division
1010 Richards Street
P.O. Box 40
Honolulu, HI 96810
808-586-2744
www.businessregistrations.com

Name Requirements

May not include name of a limited partner unless it is also the name of a general partner or the business of the limited partnership has used that name before admission of the limited partner.

Record Keeping Office Maintained Within State

Must continuously maintain office in state where required records are kept.

Required Forms

Certificate of Limited Partnership. Submit two copies to the Department of Commerce and Consumer Affairs.

Minimum Fees

$50 per partner, plus $50 if expedited service is required.

IDAHO

Secretary of State
700 W. Jefferson, Room 203
P.O. Box 83720
Boise, ID 83720-0080
208-334-2300
www.idsos.state.id.us/

Name Requirements

Must include the words "limited partnership," "L.P.," or "LP." The name may not include the words "corporation," "incorporated," or any abbreviation of these words. The name may not include the name of a limited partner unless it is also the name of a general partner or the corporate name of a corporate general partner or the business of the limited partnership has used that name before admission of the limited partner.

Record Keeping Office Maintained Within State

Must maintain required records in office of the partnership.

Required Forms

Certificate of Limited Partnership. Submit duplicate originals to the secretary of state.

Minimum Fees

$100.

ILLINOIS

Secretary of State
Limited Partnership Section
501 South Second Street
Room 357, Howlett Building
Springfield, IL 62756
217-785-8960
or
800-252-2904
www.100.state.il.us/businesscenter

Name Requirements

Must include the words "limited partnership" or "L.P." The name may not include "corporation," "corp," "incorporated," "Inc.," "company," or "co." The name may not include the name of a limited partner unless it is also the name of a general partner or the business of the limited partnership has used that name before admission of the limited partner.

Record Keeping Office Maintained Within State

Must maintain an office where required records are kept either within or outside of Illinois. If the it is outside of Illinois, then it must be at the partnership's principal place of business.

Required Forms

Certificate of Limited Partnership. Submit one original and one copy to the secretary of state.

"Filed" copy should be recorded with the recorder of the county where the register office is located.

Minimum Fees

State filing fee: $75.

Lake County Recorder: $15 for first four single-sided pages, plus $1 per side thereafter.

INDIANA

Indiana Secretary of State
Business Services Division
302 W. Washington Street, Room E018
Indianapolis, Indiana 46204
317-232-6576
www.in.gov/sic/owners/ia.html

Name Requirements

Must include the words "limited partnership" or "L.P." The name may not include "corporation," "corp," "incorporated," "Inc," "company," or "co." The name may not include the name of a limited partner unless it is also the name of a general partner or the business of the limited partnership has used that name before admission of the limited partner.

Record Keeping Office Maintained Within State

Must continuously maintain an office in state where required records are kept, which need not be the place of the partnership's business.

Required Forms

Certificate of Limited Partnership. Submit one original and one copy to the secretary of state.

Minimum Fees

$90.

IOWA

Secretary of State
Lucas Building, 1st Floor
321 E. 12th St.
Des Moines, IA 50319
515-281-5204
www.sos.state.ia.us/business/limpart.html

Name Requirements

Must include "limited partnership" or "L.P." The name may not include the words "incorporated," "corporation," or any abbreviation of these words. The name may not include the name of a limited partner unless it is also the name of a general partner or the corporate name of a corporate general partner or the business of the limited partnership has used that name before admission of the limited partner.

Record Keeping Office Maintained Within State

Must continuously maintain office in state where required records are kept.

Required Forms

Certificate of Limited Partnership. Submit one original to secretary of state.

Minimum Fees

$100.

KANSAS

Secretary of State
First Floor, Memorial Hall
120 SW 10th Ave.
Topeka, KS 66612-1594
785-296-4564
www.accesskansas.org/operating

Name Requirements

Must include the words "limited partnership" or "L.P." The name may include the words: "company," "association," "club," "foundation," "fund," "institute," "society," "union," "syndicate," "limited," "trust," or any abbreviations of these words. The name may not include the name of a limited partner unless it is also the name of a general partner or the business of the limited partnership has used that name before admission of the limited partner.

Record Keeping Office Maintained Within State

No statutory records are required to be maintained by a Kansas partnership.

Required Forms

Certificate of Limited Partnership. Submit duplicate original to the secretary of state.

Minimum Fees

$150.

KENTUCKY

Secretary of State
Corporations Division
Capitol Building Room 152
Frankfort, Kentucky 40601
502-564-2848
www.edc.state.ky.us/kyedc/bguide01.asp

Name Requirements

Must include the word "limited" or "L.P." The name may not include the name of a limited partner unless it is also the name of a general partner or the business of the limited partnership has used that name before admission of the limited partner.

Record Keeping Office Maintained Within State

Must continuously maintain office in state where required records are kept, which need not be the place of the partnership's business.

Required Forms

Certificate of Limited Partnership. Submit one original and two copies to secretary of state.

"Filed" copy must be filed with the county clerk in the county where the registered office is located.

Minimum Fees

State filing fee: $40.

County Clerk: $5.50 for first three pages, plus $1.50 each additional page.

LOUISIANA

Secretary of State
Commercial Division
P. O. Box 94125, Baton Rouge, LA 70804-9125
225-925-4704
www.sec.state.la.us/comm/comm-index.htm

Name Requirements

Must include the words "partnership in commendam," "limited partnership," or use language identifying it as a partnership. The name must not include the "name of a partner in commendam or imply that a partner in commendam is a general partner."

Record Keeping Office Within State

No statutory records are required to be maintained by a Louisiana partnership.

Required Forms

Articles of Partnership. Submit one original to the secretary of state.

Articles of Partnership and Certificate of Registry. Submit a certified copy to the Recorder of Mortgages in the parish where the partnership has its principal place of business.

Minimum Fees

State filing fee: $75 per Louisiana partner, plus $2 certification fee, plus $1 per page for each certified copy.

County fees: $13 for first two pages, plus $5 per page for each additional page, plus $5 police jury fee.

MAINE

Secretary of State
Bureau of Corporations, Elections, and Commissions
101 State House Station
Augusta, ME 04333-0101
207-624-7736
www.maine.gov/portal/business/starting.html#forms

Name Requirements

Must not include surnames of limited partners in the partnership's name, unless it is the surname of a general partner or before the time the limited partnership occurred, or the business of the partnership was carried on under a name in which his surname appeared.

Record Keeping Office Within State

No statutory records are required to be maintained by a Maine partnership.

Required Forms

Certificate of Limited Partnership. Submit an original to the secretary of state. Certificate of Confirmation of Registered Agent and Registered Office. Submit one copy to the secretary of state.

Minimum Fees

$125.

MARYLAND

Maryland Department of Assessment and Taxation
301 W. Preston Street
Room 801
Baltimore, Maryland 21202-2395
888-246-5941
or
410-767-1184
www.mdbusiness.state.md.us/business/starting/index.asp

Name Requirements

Must include the words "limited partnership" without abbreviation. The name may not include the words "corporation," "incorporated," or any abbreviation of these words. It may not include the name of a limited partner unless it is also the name of a general partner or the partnership has used that name before admission of the limited partner.

Record Keeping Office Within State

No statutory records are required to be maintained by Maryland partnerships.

Required Forms

Certificate of Limited Partnership, Consent to Serve as Resident Agent. Submit one copy of each to the Maryland Department of Assessment and Taxation.

Minimum Fees

$50, plus $30, if expedite service is required.

MASSACHUSETTS

Secretary of the Commonwealth
Corporations Division
One Ashburton Place, 17th floor
Boston, Massachusetts 02108
617-727-9640
or
617-727-2850
www.mass.gov/portal/index.jsp?pageID=cluster&c=doingbusiness

Name Requirements

Must include the words "limited partnership." The name may not include the name of a limited partner unless it is also the name of a general partner or the corporate name of a corporate general partner or the business of the partnership has been used before the admission of the limited partner.

Record Keeping Office Within State

Must continuously maintain an office in state where the required records are kept.

Required Forms

Certificate of Limited Partnership. Submit duplicate of original to secretary of the commonwealth.

Minimum Fees

$200.

MICHIGAN

Corporations Division
Michigan Department of Consumer and Industry Services
Bureau of Commercial Services
P.O. Box 30054
Lansing, MI 48909
517-241-6470
www.michigan.gov/emi/0,1303,7-102-115—-,00.html

Name Requirements

Must include the words "limited partnership" without abbreviation. The name may not include "corporation," "incorporated," or any abbreviation of these words. The name may not include the name of a limited partner unless it is also the name of a general partner or the business of the partnership has used that name before admission of the limited partner.

Record Keeping Office Within State

Must maintain an office in state where required records are kept, which need not be the place of the partnership's business.

Required Forms

Certificate of Limited Partnership. Submit original to the Corporations Division and supplement documents if necessary.

Minimum Fees

$10.

MINNESOTA

Secretary of State
Business Services
180 State Office Building
100 Constitution Avenue
Saint Paul, MN 55155
651-296-2803
www.sos.state.mn.us/business/index.html

Name Requirements

Must include the words "limited partnership," without abbreviation. The name may not include the words "corporation" or "incorporated." The name may not include the name of a limited partner unless it is also the name of a general partner or the business of the limited partnership has used that name prior to admission of the limited partner.

Record Keeping Office Within State

Must continuously maintain office in state where required records are kept, which need not be the place of the partnership's business.

Required Forms

Certificate of Limited Partnership. Submit a duplicate original to the secretary of state.

Minimum Fees

$100.

MISSISSIPPI

Mississippi Development Authority
Existing Industry and Business Division
P.O. Box 849
Jackson, Mississippi 39205-0849
601-359-3593
www.sos.state.ms.us

Name Requirements

Must include the words "limited partnership" or "L.P." The name may not include these words: "bank," "banker," "bankers," "banking," "trust company," "insurance," "trust," "corporation," "incorporated," or any combination of these words. The name may not include the name of a limited partner unless it is also the name of a general partner or the business of the limited partnership has used that name before admission of the limited partner.

Record Keeping Office Within State

Must continuously maintain office in state where required records are kept.

Required Forms

Certificate of Limited Partnership. Submit one original and one copy to the Mississippi Development Authority.

Minimum Fees

$50.

MISSOURI

Corporations Division
600 W. Main, Room 322
Jefferson City, MO 65102-0778
573-751-1310
www.sos.state.mo.us

Name Requirements

Must include "limited partnership" or "L.P." The name may not include "corporation," "incorporated," or any abbreviation of these words. The name may not include the name of a limited partner unless it is also the name of a general partner or the business of the limited partnership has used that name prior to admission of the limited partner.

Record Keeping Office Maintained Within State

Must maintain an office where required records are kept.

Required Forms

Certificate of Limited Partnership. One original and one copy to the Corporations Division.

Minimum Fees

State filing fee: $100.

MONTANA

Secretary of State
P.O. Box 202801
Helena, MT 59620-2801
406-444-3665
www.sos.state.mt.us/css

Name Requirements

Must include "limited partnership." The name may not include the name of a limited partner unless it is also the name of a general partner or the business of the limited partnership has used that name prior to admission of the limited partner.

Record Keeping Office Maintained Within State

Must continuously maintain an office in state where required records are kept.

Required Forms

Certificate of Limited Partnership. One original and one copy to secretary of state.

Minimum Fees

State filing fee: $20.

NEBRASKA

Secretary of State
Suite 1301 State Capitol
Lincoln, NE 68509
402-471-4079
www.sos.state.ne.us

Name Requirements

Must include "limited partnership" or "L.P." The name may not include "bank," "banking," "banker," "trust," "insurance," "corporation," "incorporated," or an abbreviation of these words. The name may not include the name of a limited partner unless it is also the name of a general partner or the business of the limited partnership has used that name before admission of the limited partner.

Record Keeping Office Maintained Within State

No requirements.

Required Forms

Certificate of Limited Partnership. Two copies to secretary of state.

Minimum Fees

State filing fee: $20.

NEVADA

Secretary of State
Capitol Complex
Carson City, NV 89710
702-687-5203
www.sos.state.nv.us/comm_rec/index.htm

Name Requirements

Must include "limited partnership," "L.P.," or "LP." The name may not include the name of a limited partner unless it is also the name of a general partner or the business of the limited partnership has used that name before admission of the limited partner.

Record Keeping Office Maintained Within State

Must continuously maintain an office in state where required records are kept.

Required Forms

Certificate of Limited Partnership. Two copies to the secretary of state.

Minimum Fees

State filing fee: $200, plus $3 per page recording fee.

NEW HAMPSHIRE

Secretary of State
107 N. Main Street
Concord, NH 03301-4989
603-271-3244
webster.state.nh.us/sos/

Name Requirements

Must include "limited partnership" without abbreviation. The name may not include the name of a limited partner unless it is also the name of a general partner or the business of the limited partnership has used that name before admission of the limited partner.

Record Keeping Office Maintained Within State

Must continuously maintain an office in state where required records are kept, which need not be the place of the partnership's business.

Required Forms

Certificate of Limited Partnership. Two copies to the secretary of state.

Addendum to Certificate of Limited Partnership (Form LP-1-A). One original to the secretary of state

Minimum Fees

State filing fee: $85.

NEW JERSEY

NJ Division of Revenue
P.O. Box 308
Trenton, NJ 08625-0308
609-292-9292
www.state.nj.us/njbiz

Name Requirements

Must include "limited partnership" or "L.P." The name may not include the name of a limited partner unless it is also the name of a general partner or the business of the limited partnership has used that name before admission of the limited partner.

Record Keeping Office Maintained Within State

Must keep required records at main business office.

Required Forms

Limited Partnership Certificate. One original and one copy to the New Jersey Division of Revenue.

Minimum Fees

State filing fee: $125.

NEW MEXICO

Public Regulation Commission
1120 Paseo de Peralta
PERA Bldg Rm. 536
PO Box 1269
Santa Fe, New Mexico 87504-1269
505 827-4500 voice
www.nmprc.state.nm.us/corporation.htm

Name Requirements

Must include "limited partnership" without abbreviation. The name may not include the name of a limited partner unless it is also the name of a general partner or the business of the limited partnership has used that name before admission of the limited partner.

Record Keeping Office Maintained Within State

Must maintain an office in state where required records are kept.

Required Forms

Certificate of Limited Partnership. Two originals to the Public Regulation Commission.

Minimum Fees

State filing fee: $100.

NEW YORK

NYS Department of State
Division of Corporations
41 State Street
Albany, NY 12231
518-473-2492
or
518-474-6200
www.dos.state.ny.us/corp/corpwww.html

Name Requirements

Must include "Limited Partnership" or "L.P." The name may not include "board of trade," "chamber of commerce," "community renewal," "state police," "state trooper," "tenant relocation," "urban development," "urban relocation," or any abbreviation of these phrases. May not include certain words or any abbreviation of these words without approval attached to the certificate of limited partnership from the appropriate office, either the Superintendent of Banks, Superintendent of Insurance, or the State Department of Social Services. May not include "doctor," "lawyer," or an abbreviation of these words unless used to indicate the practice of medicine or law. May not include the word or abbreviation of "exchange" without the approval attached to the certificate of limited partnership of the attorney general.

Record Keeping Office Maintained Within State

Must maintain required records.

Required Forms

Certificate of Limited Partnership. One original to the NYS Department of State. Within 120 days of filing, must publish one copy or notice once a week for six successive weeks in two newspapers in the county where the office of the limited partnership is located.

Minimum Fees

State filing fee: $200, plus $25 per affidavit of publication from each of the two county newspapers.

Publication: Costs vary according to county and newspaper ($900-$2500).

NORTH CAROLINA

Corporations Division
P.O. Box 29622
Raleigh, NC 27626-0622
919-807-2225
www.secretary.state.nc.us/Corporations/

Name Requirements

Must include "limited partnership" without abbreviation. The name may not include the name of a limited partner unless it is also the name of a general partner or the business of the limited partnership has used that name before admission of the limited partner.

Record Keeping Office Maintained Within State

Must continuously maintain an office in state where required records are kept, which need not be the place of the partnership's business.

Required Forms

Certificate of Domestic Limited Partnership. One original and one conformed copy to the Corporations Division. The copy must be recorded in the register of deeds in the county where the limited partnership has its registered office within sixty days of confirmation.

Minimum Fees

State filing fee: $50.

County recording fees vary.

NORTH DAKOTA

State of North Dakota
Secretary of State
600 E. Boulevard Ave. Dept. 108
Bismark, ND 58505-0500
701-328-4284 or
800-352-0867 ext. 4284
www.state.nd.us/sec/

Name Requirements

Must include "limited partnership" without abbreviation. The name may not include "company," "corporation," "incorporated," or an abbreviation of such words. The name may not include the name of a limited partner unless it is also the name of a general partner or the business of the limited partnership has used that name before admission of the limited partner.

Record Keeping Office Maintained Within State

Must continuously maintain an office in state where required records are kept.

Required Forms

Certificate of Limited Partnership. Duplicate originals to the secretary of state.

Minimum Fees

State filing fee: $100.

OHIO

Secretary of State
Corporations Division
180 E. Broad Street, 16th Floor
Columbus, OH 43215
614-466-3910
www.state.oh.us/sos

Name Requirements

Must include "Limited Partnership," "L.P.," "Limited," or "Ltd." The name may not include the name of a limited partner unless it is also the name of a general partner or the business of the limited partnership has used that name before admission of the limited partner.

Record Keeping Office Maintained Within State

Must maintain required records at main office, which need not be in Ohio.

Required Forms

Certificate of Limited Partnership. One copy to the secretary of state.

Minimum Fees

State filing fee: $125, plus $100 for expedited services.

OKLAHOMA

Secretary of State
Business Filing Department
2300 N. Lincoln Blvd., Room 101
Oklahoma City, OK 73105-4897
405-521-3912
www.sos.state.ok.us

Name Requirements

Must include "limited partnership," "L.P.," or "LP." The name may not include the name of a limited partner unless it is also the name of a general partner or the business of the limited partnership has used that name before admission of the limited partner.

Record Keeping Office Maintained Within State

Must continuously maintain an office in state where required records are kept.

Required Forms

Certificate of Limited Partnership. Two originals to the secretary of state.

Minimum Fees

State filing fee: $100.

OREGON

State of Oregon
Corporation Division
255 Capitol Street NE, Suite 151
Salem, Oregon 97310-1327
503-986-2200
www.Filinginoregon.com

Name Requirements

Must include, without abbreviation, "limited partnership." The name may not include "corporation" or "incorporated" or any abbreviation of these words. The name may not include the name of a limited partner unless it is also the name of a general partner or the business of the limited partnership has used that name before admission of the limited partner.

Record Keeping Office Maintained Within State

Must continuously maintain an office in state where required records are kept.

Required Forms

Certificate of Limited Partnership. One original and one conformed copy to the Corporation Division.

Minimum Fees

State filing fee: $20.

PENNSYLVANIA

Department of State
Corporation Bureau
P.O. Box 8722
Harrisburg, PA 17105-8722
717-787-1057
www.state.pa.us

Name Requirements

None.

Record Keeping Office Maintained Within State

Must maintain required records at registered or main office.

Required Forms

Certificate of Limited Partnership. One original and one copy to the department of state.

Minimum Fees

State filing fee: $100.

RHODE ISLAND

Secretary of State
100 N. Main Street
Providence, RI 02903
401-222-3040
www.corps.state.ri.us/corporations.htm

Name Requirements

Must include "limited partnership" or "L.P." The name may not include the name of a limited partner unless it is also the name of a general partner or the business of the limited partnership has used that name before admission of the limited partner.

Record Keeping Office Maintained Within State

Must continuously maintain an office in state where required records are kept.

Required Forms

Certificate of Limited Partnership. Duplicate originals to the secretary of state.

Minimum Fees

State filing fee: $100.

SOUTH CAROLINA

Secretary of State
P.O. Box 11350
Columbia, SC 29211
803-734-2158
www.scsos.com

Name Requirements

Must include "limited partnership," "L.P.," or "LP." The name may not include "Limited" or "Ltd." The name may not include the name of a limited partner unless it is also the name of a general partner or the business of the limited partnership has used that name before admission of the limited partner.

Record Keeping Office Maintained Within State

Must continuously maintain an office in state where required records are kept.

Required Forms

Certificate of Limited Partnership. Two copies to the secretary of state.

Minimum Fees

State filing fee: $10.

SOUTH DAKOTA

Secretary of State
State Capital
500 E. Capital Street
Pierre, SD 57501
605-773-4845
www.state.sd.us/sos/sos.htm

Name Requirements

Must include, without abbreviation, "Limited Partnership." The name may not include the name of a limited partner unless it is also the name of a general partner or the business of the limited partnership has used that name before admission of the limited partner.

Record Keeping Office Maintained Within State

Must continuously maintain an office in state where required records are kept.

Required Forms

Certificate of Limited Partnership. One original and one conformed copy to the secretary of state.

Minimum Fees

State filing fee: $10.

TENNESSEE

Department of State
Corporate Filings
312 Eighth Avenue North
6th Floor, William R. Snodgrass Tower
Nashville, TN 37243
615-741-2286
www.state.tn.us/sos/service.htm

NAME REQUIREMENTS

Must include "limited partnership" or "L.P." The name may include "association," "club," "company," "foundation," "fund," "institute," "society," "union," "syndicate," "limited," or "trust." The name may not include "corporation," "incorporated," or an abbreviation of these words.

RECORD KEEPING OFFICE MAINTAINED WITHIN STATE

Required records must be kept in the registered office.

REQUIRED FORMS

Certificate of Limited Partnership. One original to the Department of State. Must also be recorded in the register's office in the county where the main office of the limited partnership is located.

MINIMUM FEES

State filing fee: $100.

County recording fees vary.

TEXAS

Corporations Section
Statutory Filings Division
Office of the Secretary of State
P.O. Box 13697
Austin, Texas 78711-3697
512-463-5555
www.sos.state.tx.us/corp/index.shtml

Name Requirements

Must include "Limited Partnership," "Limited," "L.P.," or "Ltd." The name may not include the name of a limited partner unless it is also the name of a general partner or the business of the limited partnership has used that name before admission of the limited partner.

Record Keeping Office Maintained Within State

Must maintain required records in main office or make them available within five days of receipt of a request from a partner or an assignee of a partnership interest.

Required Forms

Certificate of Limited Partnership. Duplicated originals to the Corporations Section.

Minimum Fees

State filing fee: $750.

UTAH

Department of Commerce
Division of Corporations and Commercial Code
S.M. Box 146705
Salt Lake City, UT 84114-6705
801-530-4849
www.utah.gov/business/generalinfo.html

Name Requirements

Must include "limited partnership," "limited," "L.P.," or "Ltd." The name may not include "association," "corporation," "incorporated," or an abbreviation of these words or words of similar nature in other languages. The name may not include the name of a limited partner unless it is also the name of a general partner or the business of the limited partnership has used that name before admission of the limited partner.

Record Keeping Office Maintained Within State

Must maintain required records at main office where the limited partnership is located.

Required Forms

Certificate of Limited Partnership. One original and one copy to the Division of Corporations and Commercial Code.

Minimum Fees

State filing fee: $50, plus $25 if expedited service is required.

VERMONT

Secretary of State's Office
81 River Street, Drawer 09
Montpelier, VT 05609
802-828-2386
www.sec.state.vt.us/corps/corpindex.htm

Name Requirements

The name may not include the name of a limited partner unless it is also the name of a general partner or the business of the limited partnership has used that name before admission of the limited partner.

Record Keeping Office Maintained Within State

N/A

Required Forms

Certificate of Limited Partnership. One original to the town clerk in the town where the main office of the limited partnership is located.

Trade Name Registration. One original to the secretary of state. One "validated" copy to the town clerk.

Minimum Fees

State filing fee: $20.

Town clerk: $6 per page.

VIRGINIA

Clerk of the State Corporation Commission
P.O. Box 1197
Richmond, Virginia 23218-1197
804-371-9733
www.state.va.us/scc/division/clk

NAME REQUIREMENTS

Must include "limited partnership" or "L.P." The name may not include "Corporation," "Incorporated," "Corp.," or "Inc." The name may not include the name of a limited partner unless it is also the name of a general partner or the business of the limited partnership has used that name before admission of the limited partner.

RECORD KEEPING OFFICE MAINTAINED WITHIN STATE

Must continuously maintain an office in state where required records are kept.

REQUIRED FORMS

Certificate of Limited Partnership. One copy to the State Corporation Commission.

MINIMUM FEES

State filing fee: $100.

WASHINGTON

Secretary of State
Corporations Division
P.O. Box 40234
Olympia, WA 98504-0234
360-753-7115
www.secstate.wa.gov/corps

Name Requirements

Must include "Limited Partnership" or "L.P." The name may not include "bank," "banking," "banker," "trust," "cooperative," or any combination of the words "industrial" and "loan"; or any combination of two or more of the words "building," "savings," "loan," "home," "association," and "society"; or any other words or phrases prohibited by Washington law. The name may not include the name of a limited partner unless it is also the name of a general partner or the business of the limited partnership has used that name before admission of the limited partner.

Record Keeping Office Maintained Within State

Must continuously maintain an office in state where required records are kept.

Required Forms

Certificate of Limited Partnership. One copy to the secretary of state with the Index Sheet. (Contact the secretary of state's office for more information about the Index Sheet.)

Minimum Fees

State filing fee: $175 with index, $225 without.

WEST VIRGINIA

Secretary of State
Building 1, Suite 157-K
1900 Kanawha Boulevard East
Charleston, WV 25305-0770
304-558-8000
www.state.wv.us/sos

NAME REQUIREMENTS

Must include, without abbreviation, "limited partnership." The name may not include "engineers" or "engineering" unless the limited partnership practices professional engineering. The name may not include the name of a limited partner unless it is also the name of a general partner or the business of the limited partnership has used that name before admission of the limited partner.

RECORD KEEPING OFFICE MAINTAINED WITHIN STATE

Must continuously maintain an office in state where required records are kept, which need not be the place of the partnership's business.

REQUIRED FORMS

Certificate of Limited Partnership. Two originals to the secretary of state. Submit the certificate from the secretary of state or a certified copy to the clerk of the county commission of the county where the record keeping office is located.

MINIMUM FEES

State filing fee: $100, plus $25 attorney-in-fact fee prorated.

County recording fee: $2 for the first two pages, $1 for each additional page.

WISCONSIN

Department of Financial Institutions
Division of Corporate & Consumer Services
P.O. Box 7846
Madison, WI 53707-7846
608-261-7577
www.wisconsin.gov

Name Requirements

Must include, without abbreviation, "limited partnership." The name may not include the name of a limited partner unless it is also the name of a general partner or the business of the limited partnership has used that name before admission of the limited partner.

Record Keeping Office Maintained Within State

Must continuously maintain an office in state where required records are kept.

Required Forms

Certificate of Limited Partnership. Two originals to the Department of Financial Institutions.

Minimum Fees

State filing fee: $70.

WYOMING

Secretary of State
State Capitol Building
Cheyenne, WY 82002-0020
307-777-7311
or
307-777-5339
soswy.state.wy.us/corporat/corporat.htm

Name Requirements

Must include, without abbreviation, "limited partnership." The name may not include the name of a limited partner unless it is also the name of a general partner or the business of the limited partnership has used that name before admission of the limited partner.

Record Keeping Office Maintained Within State

Must continuously maintain an office in state where required records are kept.

Required Forms

Certificate of Limited Partnership. Two originals to the secretary of state.

Minimum Fees

State filing fee: $100 filing fee.

Appendix C

Valid Purposes for a Family Limited Partnership

In order to receive the tax benefits of being a limited partnership, it is essential that the Internal Revenue Service deem your FLP as valid. Following is a list of FLP business purposes that have been recognized as valid by the IRS. You will set forth your FLP's business purpose in both your limited **Partnership Agreement** and your **Certificate of Partnership.**

A. Make money

B. Increase wealth

C. Consolidate fractional interests

   1. Increase wealth
   2. More efficient management of assets
   3. Better negotiating position
   4. Make dealing with third parties easier
   5. Reduce or eliminate disputes between partners

D. Manage and develop real estate

E. Avoid two layers of taxation on profits

F. Reduce state taxes

G. Reduce income taxes

H. Facilitate annual gifting

I. Control cash flow to limited partners

J. Provide a buy-sell arrangement

K. Resolve disputes privately

L. Provide for mediation and arbitration

   1. Mediation

   2. Arbitration

   3. Reduces emotional stress among partnership members

M. Provide confidentiality

N. Avoid living probate

O. Avoid death probate

P. Establish an order of succession

Q. Restrict the right of non-partners to acquire interests

R. Prevent transfers of partnership interests because of failed marriages

S. Prevent commingling of the assets of gift recipients

T. Make it difficult to withdraw

U. Protect against future creditors of partners

V. Provide asset protection

   1. Reduce the amount of lawsuit settlements

   2. Reduce the number of lawsuits

   3. Protect against exemplary damages

   4. Protect against the bankruptcy of insurance carriers

   5. Save on insurance costs

W. Allow for more flexible business planning

1. More flexible than a trust

a. Can be amended

b. Better income tax returns

2. More flexible than a C corporation

a. Two layers of taxation

b. Restricted transferability

c. Limited life

d. Tax consequences on formation

e. Tax consequences on dissolution

f. State franchise tax

3. More flexible than a limited liability company

X. Promote knowledge of family assets

Y. Qualify for the family business exclusion in the Taxpayer Relief Act of 1997

Z. Reduce the impact of income in respect of a decedent

AA. Partnership income is not subject to self-employment tax

BB. Partnership income is not subject to Medicare tax

CC. Financial operation

DD. Keep family members close

Appendix D
Uniform Limited Partnership Act

Each state has adopted its own version of the Uniform Limited Partnership Act. You should use your state's modified version as your legal authority. However, you may use ULPA as a general reference for understanding partnership concepts, such as the requirements for writing and amending your Certificate of Limited Partnership. You may also be interested in how your state modified ULPA from its original form.

UNIFORM LIMITED PARTNERSHIP ACT (1976) WITH 1985 AMENDMENTS

ARTICLE 1
GENERAL PROVISIONS

SECTION 101. DEFINITIONS. As used in this Act, unless the context otherwise requires:

(1) "Certificate of limited partnership" means the certificate referred to in Section 201, and the certificate as amended or restated.

(2) "Contribution" means any cash, property, services rendered, or a promissory note or other binding obligation to contribute cash or property or to perform services, which a partner contributes to a limited partnership in his capacity as a partner.

(3) "Event of withdrawal of a general partner" means an event that causes a person to cease to be a general partner as provided in Section 402.

(4) "Foreign limited partnership" means a partnership formed under the laws of any state other than this State and having as partners one or more general partners and one or more limited partners.

(5) "General partner" means a person who has been admitted to a limited partnership as a general partner in accordance with the partnership agreement and named in the certificate of limited partnership as a general partner.

(6) "Limited partner" means a person who has been admitted to a limited partnership as a limited partner in accordance with the partnership agreement.

(7) "Limited partnership" and "domestic limited partnership" mean a partnership formed by two or more persons under the laws of this State and having one or more general partners and one or more limited partners.

(8) "Partner" means a limited or general partner.

(9) "Partnership agreement" means any valid agreement, written or oral, of the partners as to the affairs of a limited partnership and the conduct of its business.

(10) "Partnership interest" means a partner's share of the profits and losses of a limited partnership and the right to receive distributions of partnership assets.

(11) "Person" means a natural person, partnership, limited partnership (domestic or foreign), trust, estate, association, or corporation.

(12) "State" means a state, territory, or possession of the United States, the District of Columbia, or the Commonwealth of Puerto Rico.

SECTION 102. NAME. The name of each limited partnership as set forth in its certificate of limited partnership:

(1) shall contain without abbreviation the words "limited partnership";

(2) may not contain the name of a limited partner unless

(i) it is also the name of a general partner or the corporate name of a corporate general partner, or

(ii) the business of the limited partnership had been carried on under that name before the admission of that limited partner;

(3) may not be the same as, or deceptively similar to, the name of any corporation or limited partnership organized under the laws of this State or licensed or registered as a foreign corporation or limited partnership in this State; and

(4) may not contain the following words [here insert prohibited words].

SECTION 103. RESERVATION OF NAME.

(a) The exclusive right to the use of a name may be reserved by:

(1) any person intending to organize a limited partnership under this Act and to adopt that name;

(2) any domestic limited partnership or any foreign limited partnership registered in this State which, in either case, intends to adopt that name;

(3) any foreign limited partnership intending to register in this State and adopt that name; and

(4) any person intending to organize a foreign limited partnership and intending to have it register in this State and adopt that name.

(b) The reservation shall be made by filing with the Secretary of State an application, executed by the applicant, to reserve a specified name. If the Secretary of State finds that the name is available for use by a domestic or foreign limited partnership, he or she shall reserve the name for the exclusive use of the applicant for a period of 120 days. Once having so reserved a name, the same applicant may not again reserve the same name until more than 60 days after the expiration of the last 120-day period for which that applicant reserved that name. The right to the exclusive use of a reserved name may be transferred to any other person by filing in the office of the Secretary of State a notice of the transfer, executed by the applicant for whom the name was reserved and specifying the name and address of the transferee.

SECTION 104. SPECIFIED OFFICE AND AGENT. Each limited partnership shall continuously maintain in this State:

(1) an office, which may but need not be a place of its business in this State, at which shall be kept the records required by Section 105 to be maintained; and

(2) an agent for service of process on the limited partnership, which agent must be an individual resident of this State, a domestic corporation, or a foreign corporation authorized to do business in this State.

SECTION 105. RECORDS TO BE KEPT.(a) Each limited partnership shall keep at the office referred to in Section 104(1) the following:

(1) a current list of the full name and last known business address of each partner separately identifying the general partners (in alphabetical order) and the limited partners (in alphabetical order);

(2) a copy of the certificate of limited partnership and all certificates of amendment thereto, together with executed copies of any powers of attorney pursuant to which any certificate has been executed;

(3) copies of the limited partnership's federal, state and local income tax returns and reports, if any, for the three most recent years and;

(4) copies of any then effective written partnership agreements and of any financial statements of the limited partnership for the three most recent years; and

(5) unless contained in a written partnership agreement, a writing setting out:

(i) the amount of cash and a description and statement of the agreed value of the other property or services contributed by each partner and which each partner has agreed to contribute;

(ii) the times at which or events on the happening of which any additional contributions agreed to be made by each partner are to be made;

(iii) any right of a partner to receive, or of a general partner to make, distributions to a partner which include a return of all or any part of the partner's contribution; and

(iv) any events upon the happening of which the limited partnership is to be dissolved and its affairs wound up.

(b) Records kept under this section are subject to inspection and copying at the reasonable request and at the expense of any partner during ordinary business hours.

SECTION 106. NATURE OF BUSINESS. A limited partnership may carry on any business that a partnership without limited partners may carry on except [here designate prohibited activities].

SECTION 107. BUSINESS TRANSACTIONS OF PARTNER WITH PARTNERSHIP. Except as provided in the partnership agreement, a partner may lend money to and transact other business with the limited partnership and, subject to other applicable law, has the same rights and obligations with respect thereto as a person who is not a partner.

ARTICLE 2

FORMATION: CERTIFICATE OF LIMITED PARTNERSHIP

SECTION 201. CERTIFICATE OF LIMITED PARTNERSHIP.

(a) In order to form a limited partnership, a certificate of limited partnership must be executed and filed in the office of the Secretary of State. The certificate shall set forth:

(1) the name of the limited partnership;

(2) the address of the office and the name and address of the agent for service of process required to be maintained by Section 104;

(3) the name and the business address of each general partner;

(4) the latest date upon which the limited partnership is to dissolve; and

(5) any other matters the general partners determine to include therein.

(b) A limited partnership is formed at the time of the filing of the certificate of limited partnership in the office of the Secretary of State or at any later time specified in the certificate of limited partnership if, in either case, there has been substantial compliance with the requirements of this section.

SECTION 202. AMENDMENT TO CERTIFICATE.

(a) A certificate of limited partnership is amended by filing a certificate of amendment thereto in the office of the Secretary of State. The certificate shall set forth:

(1) the name of the limited partnership;

(2) the date of filing the certificate; and

(3) the amendment to the certificate.

(b) Within 30 days after the happening of any of the following events, an amendment to a certificate of limited partnership reflecting the occurrence of the event or events shall be filed:

(1) the admission of a new general partner;

(2) the withdrawal of a general partner; or

(3) the continuation of the business under Section 801 after an event of withdrawal of a general partner.

(c) A general partner who becomes aware that any statement in a certificate of limited partnership was false when made or that any arrangements or other facts described have changed, making the certificate inaccurate in any respect, shall promptly amend the certificate.

(d) A certificate of limited partnership may be amended at any time for any other proper purpose the general partners determine.

(e) No person has any liability because an amendment to a certificate of limited partnership has not been filed to reflect the occurrence of any event referred to in subsection (b) of this section if the amendment is filed within the 30-day period specified in subsection (b).

(f) A restated certificate of limited partnership may be executed and filed in the same manner as a certificate of amendment.

SECTION 203. CANCELLATION OF CERTIFICATE. A certificate of limited partnership shall be cancelled upon the dissolution and the commencement of winding up of the partnership or at any other time there are no limited partners. A certificate of cancellation shall be filed in the office of the Secretary of State and set forth:

(1) the name of the limited partnership;

(2) the date of filing of its certificate of limited partnership;

(3) the reason for filing the certificate of cancellation;

(4) the effective date (which shall be a date certain) of cancellation if it is not to be effective upon the filing of the certificate; and

(5) any other information the general partners filing the certificate determine.

SECTION 204. EXECUTION OF CERTIFICATES.

(a) Each certificate required by this Article to be filed in the office of the Secretary of State shall be executed in the following manner:

(1) an original certificate of limited partnership must be signed by all general partners;

(2) a certificate of amendment must be signed by at least one general partner and by each other general partner designated in the certificate as a new general partner; and

(3) a certificate of cancellation must be signed by all general partners.(b) Any person may sign a certificate by an attorney-in-fact, but a power of attorney to sign a certificate relating to the admission of a general partner must specifically describe the admission.(c) The execution of a certificate by a general partner constitutes an affirmation under the penalties of perjury that the facts stated therein are true.

SECTION 205. EXECUTION BY JUDICIAL ACT. If a person required by Section 204 to execute any certificate fails or refuses to do so, any other person who is adversely affected by the failure or refusal, may petition the designate the appropriate court to direct the execution of the certificate. If the court finds that it is proper for the certificate to be executed and that any person so designated has failed or refused to execute the certificate, it shall order the Secretary of State to record an appropriate certificate.

SECTION 206. FILING IN OFFICE OF SECRETARY OF STATE.

(a) Two signed copies of the certificate of limited partnership and of any certificates of amendment or cancellation (or of any judicial decree of amendment or cancellation) shall be delivered to the Secretary of State. A person who executes a certificate as an agent or fiduciary need not exhibit evidence of his or her authority as a prerequisite to filing. Unless the Secretary of State finds that any certificate does not conform to law, upon receipt of all filing fees required by law he or she shall:

(1) endorse on each duplicate original the word "Filed" and the day, month and year of the filing thereof;

(2) file one duplicate original in his or her office; and

(3) return the other duplicate original to the person who filed it or his or her representative.

(b) Upon the filing of a certificate of amendment (or judicial decree of amendment) in the office of the Secretary of State, the certificate of limited partnership shall be amended as set forth therein, and upon the effective date of a certificate of cancellation (or a judicial decree thereof), the certificate of limited partnership is cancelled.

SECTION 207. LIABILITY FOR FALSE STATEMENT IN CERTIFICATE. If any certificate of limited partnership or certificate of amendment or cancellation contains a false statement, one who suffers loss by reliance on the statement may recover damages for the loss from:

(1) any person who executes the certificate, or causes another to execute it on his behalf, and knew, and any general partner who knew or should have known, the statement to be false at the time the certificate was executed; and

(2) any general partner who thereafter knows or should have known that any arrangement or other fact described in the certificate has changed, making the statement inaccurate in any respect within a sufficient time before the statement was relied upon reasonably to have enabled that general partner to cancel or amend the certificate, or to file a petition for its cancellation or amendment under Section 205.

SECTION 208. SCOPE OF NOTICE. The fact that a certificate of limited partnership is on file in the office of the Secretary of State is notice that the partnership is a limited partnership and the persons designated therein as general partners are general partners, but it is not notice of any other fact.

SECTION 209. DELIVERY OF CERTIFICATES TO LIMITED PARTNERS. Upon the return by the Secretary of State pursuant to Section 206 of a certificate marked "Filed", the general partners shall promptly deliver or mail a copy of the certificate of limited partnership and each certificate of amendment or cancellation to each limited partner unless the partnership agreement provides otherwise.

ARTICLE 3

LIMITED PARTNERS

SECTION 301. ADMISSION OF LIMITED PARTNERS.

(a) A person becomes a limited partner:

(1) at the time the limited partnership is formed; or

(2) at any later time specified in the records of the limited partnership for becoming a limited partner.

(b) After the filing of a limited partnership's original certificate of limited partnership, a person may be admitted as an additional limited partner:

(1) in the case of a person acquiring a partnership interest directly from the limited partnership, upon compliance with the partnership agreement or, if the partnership agreement does not so provide, upon the written consent of all partners; and

(2) in the case of an assignee of a partnership interest of a partner who has the power, as provided in Section 704, to grant the assignee the right to become

a limited partner, upon the exercise of that power and compliance with any conditions limiting the grant or exercise of the power.

SECTION 302. VOTING. Subject to Section 303, the partnership agreement may grant to all or a specified group of the limited partners the right to vote (on a per capita or other basis) upon any matter.

SECTION 303. LIABILITY TO THIRD PARTIES.

(a) Except as provided in subsection (d), a limited partner is not liable for the obligations of a limited partnership unless he or she is also a general partner or, in addition to the exercise of his or her rights and powers as a limited partner, he or she participates in the control of the business. However, if the limited partner participates in the control of the business, he or she is liable only to persons who transact business with the limited partnership reasonably believing, based upon the limited partner's conduct, that the limited partner is a general partner.

(b) A limited partner does not participate in the control of the business within the meaning of subsection (a) solely by doing one or more of the following:

(1) being a contractor for or an agent or employee of the limited partnership or of a general partner or being an officer, director, or shareholder of a general partner that is a corporation;

(2) consulting with and advising a general partner with respect to the business of the limited partnership;

(3) acting as surety for the limited partnership or guaranteeing or assuming one or more specific obligations of the limited partnership;

(4) taking any action required or permitted by law to bring or pursue a derivative action in the right of the limited partnership;

(5) requesting or attending a meeting of partners;

(6) proposing, approving, or disapproving, by voting or otherwise, one or more of the following matters:

(i) the dissolution and winding up of the limited partnership;

(ii) the sale, exchange, lease, mortgage, pledge, or other transfer of all or substantially all of the assets of the limited partnership;

(iii) the incurrence of indebtedness by the limited partnership other than in the ordinary course of its business;

(iv) a change in the nature of the business;

(v) the admission or removal of a general partner;

(vi) the admission or removal of a limited partner;

(vii) a transaction involving an actual or potential conflict of interest between a general partner and the limited partnership or the limited partners;

(viii) an amendment to the partnership agreement or certificate of limited partnership; or

(ix) matters related to the business of the limited partnership not otherwise enumerated in this subsection (b), which the partnership agreement states in writing may be subject to the approval or disapproval of limited partners;

(7) winding up the limited partnership pursuant to Section 803; or

(8) exercising any right or power permitted to limited partners under this Act and not specifically enumerated in this subsection (b).(c) The enumeration in subsection (b) does not mean that the possession or exercise of any other powers by a limited partner constitutes participation by him or her in the business of the limited partnership.(d) A limited partner who knowingly permits his or her name to be used in the name of the limited partnership, except under circumstances permitted by Section 102(2), is liable to creditors who extend credit to the limited partnership without actual knowledge that the limited partner is not a general partner.

SECTION 304. PERSON ERRONEOUSLY BELIEVING HIMSELF OR HERSELF LIMITED PARTNER.(a) Except as provided in subsection (b), a person who makes a contribution to a business enterprise and erroneously but in good faith believes that he or she has become a limited partner in the enterprise is not a general partner in the enterprise and is not bound by its obligations by reason of making the contribution, receiving distributions from the enterprise, or exercising any rights of a limited partner, if, on ascertaining the mistake, he or she:

(1) causes an appropriate certificate of limited partnership or a certificate of amendment to be executed and filed; or

(2) withdraws from future equity participation in the enterprise by executing and filing in the office of the Secretary of State a certificate declaring withdrawal under this section.

(b) A person who makes a contribution of the kind described in subsection (a) is liable as a general partner to any third party who transacts business with the enterprise

(i) before the person withdraws and an appropriate certificate is filed to show withdrawal, or

(ii) before an appropriate certificate is filed to show that he or she is not a general partner, but in either case only if the third party actually believed in good faith that the person was a general partner at the time of the transaction.

SECTION 305. INFORMATION. Each limited partner has the right to:

(1) inspect and copy any of the partnership records required to be maintained by Section 105; and

(2) obtain from the general partners from time to time upon reasonable demand

(i) true and full information regarding the state of the business and financial condition of the limited partnership,

(ii) promptly after becoming available, a copy of the limited partnership's federal, state and local income tax returns for each year, and

(iii) other information regarding the affairs of the limited partnership as is just and reasonable.

ARTICLE 4

GENERAL PARTNERS

SECTION 401. ADMISSION OF ADDITIONAL GENERAL PARTNERS. After the filing of a limited partnership's original certificate of limited partnership, additional general partners may be admitted as provided in writing in the partnership agreement or, if the partnership agreement does not provide in writing for the admission of additional general partners, with the written consent of all partners.

SECTION 402. EVENTS OF WITHDRAWAL. Except as approved by the specific written consent of all partners at the time, a person ceases to be a general partner of a limited partnership upon the happening of any of the following events:

(1) the general partner withdraws from the limited partnership as provided in Section 602;

(2) the general partner ceases to be a member of the limited partnership as provided in Section 702;

(3) the general partner is removed as a general partner in accordance with the partnership agreement;

(4) unless otherwise provided in writing in the partnership agreement, the general partner:

(i) makes an assignment for the benefit of creditors;

(ii) files a voluntary petition in bankruptcy;

(iii) is adjudicated a bankrupt or insolvent;

(iv) files a petition or answer seeking for himself or herself any reorganization, arrangement, composition, readjustment, liquidation, dissolution or similar relief under any statute, law, or regulation;

(v) files an answer or other pleading admitting or failing to contest the material allegations of a petition filed against him or her in any proceeding of this nature; or

(vi) seeks, consents to, or acquiesces in the appointment of a trustee, receiver, or liquidator of the general partner or of all or any substantial part of his or her properties;

(5) unless otherwise provided in writing in the partnership agreement, [120] days after the commencement of any proceeding against the general partner seeking reorganization, arrangement, composition, readjustment, liquidation, dissolution or similar relief under any statute, law, or regulation, the proceeding has not been dismissed, or if within [90] days after the appointment without his or her consent or acquiescence of a trustee, receiver, or liquidator of the general partner or of all or any substantial part of his or her properties, the appointment is not vacated or stayed or within [90] days after the expiration of any such stay, the appointment is not vacated;(6) in the case of a general partner who is a natural person,

(i) his or her death; or

(ii) the entry of an order by a court of competent jurisdiction adjudicating him or her incompetent to manage his or her person or his or her estate;

(7) in the case of a general partner who is acting as a general partner by virtue of being a trustee of a trust, the termination of the trust (but not merely the substitution of a new trustee);

(8) in the case of a general partner that is a separate partnership, the dissolution and commencement of winding up of the separate partnership;

(9) in the case of a general partner that is a corporation, the filing of a certificate of dissolution, or its equivalent, for the corporation or the revocation of its charter; or

(10) in the case of an estate, the distribution by the fiduciary of the estate's entire interest in the partnership.

SECTION 403. GENERAL POWERS AND LIABILITIES.

(a) Except as provided in this Act or in the partnership agreement, a general partner of a limited partnership has the rights and powers and is subject to the restrictions of a partner in a partnership without limited partners.

(b) Except as provided in this Act, a general partner of a limited partnership has the liabilities of a partner in a partnership without limited partners to persons other than the partnership and the other partners. Except as provided in this Act or in the partnership agreement, a general partner of a limited partnership has the liabilities of a partner in a partnership without limited partners to the partnership and to the other partners.

SECTION 404. CONTRIBUTIONS BY GENERAL PARTNER. A general partner of a limited partnership may make contributions to the partnership and share in the profits and losses of, and in distributions from, the limited partnership as a general partner. A general partner also may make contributions to and share in profits, losses, and distributions as a limited partner. A person who is both a general partner and a limited partner has the rights and powers, and is subject to the restrictions and liabilities, of a general partner and, except as provided in the partnership agreement, also has the powers, and is subject to the restrictions, of a limited partner to the extent of his or her participation in the partnership as a limited partner.

SECTION 405. VOTING. The partnership agreement may grant to all or certain identified general partners the right to vote (on a per capita or any other basis), separately or with all or any class of the limited partners, on any matter.

ARTICLE 5

FINANCE

SECTION 501. FORM OF CONTRIBUTION. The contribution of a partner may be in cash, property, or services rendered, or a promissory note or other obligation to contribute cash or property or to perform services.

SECTION 502. LIABILITY FOR CONTRIBUTION.(a) A promise by a limited partner to contribute to the limited partnership is not enforceable unless set out in a writing signed by the limited partner.

(b) Except as provided in the partnership agreement, a partner is obligated to the limited partnership to perform any enforceable promise to contribute cash or property or to perform services, even if he or she is unable to perform because of death, disability, or any other reason. If a partner does not make the required contribution of property or services, he or she is obligated at the option of the limited partnership to contribute cash equal to that portion of the value, as stated in the partnership records required to be kept pursuant to Section 105, of the stated contribution which has not been made.

(c) Unless otherwise provided in the partnership agreement, the obligation of a partner to make a contribution or return money or other property paid or distributed in violation of this Act may be compromised only by consent of all partners. Notwithstanding the compromise, a creditor of a limited partnership who extends credit or otherwise acts in reliance on that obligation after the partner signs a writing which reflects the obligation and before the amendment or cancellation thereof to reflect the compromise may enforce the original obligation.

SECTION 503. SHARING OF PROFITS AND LOSSES. The profits and losses of a limited partnership shall be allocated among the partners, and among classes of partners, in the manner provided in writing in the partnership agreement. If the partnership agreement does not so provide in writing, profits and losses shall be allocated on the basis of the value, as stated in the partnership records required to be kept pursuant to Section 105, of the contributions made by each partner to the extent they have been received by the partnership and have not been returned.

SECTION 504. SHARING OF DISTRIBUTIONS. Distributions of cash or other assets of a limited partnership shall be allocated among the partners and among classes of partners in the manner provided in writing in the partnership agreement. If the partnership agreement does not so provide in writing, distributions shall be made on the basis of the value, as stated in the partnership records required to be kept pursuant to Section 105, of the contributions made by each partner to the extent they have been received by the partnership and have not been returned.

ARTICLE 6

DISTRIBUTIONS AND WITHDRAWAL

SECTION 601. INTERIM DISTRIBUTIONS. Except as provided in this Article, a partner is entitled to receive distributions from a limited partnership before his or her withdrawal from the limited partnership and before the dissolution and winding up thereof to the extent and at the times or upon the happening of the events specified in the partnership agreement.

SECTION 602. WITHDRAWAL OF GENERAL PARTNER. A general partner may withdraw from a limited partnership at any time by giving written notice to the other partners, but if the withdrawal violates the partnership agreement, the limited partnership may recover from the withdrawing general partner damages for breach of the partnership agreement and offset the damages against the amount otherwise distributable to him or her.

SECTION 603. WITHDRAWAL OF LIMITED PARTNER. A limited partner may withdraw from a limited partnership at the time or upon the happening of events specified in writing in the partnership agreement. If the agreement does not specify in writing the time or the events upon the happening of which a limited partner may withdraw or a definite time for the dissolution and winding up of the limited partnership, a limited partner may withdraw upon not less than six months' prior written notice to each general partner at his or her address on the books of the limited partnership at its office in this State.

SECTION 604. DISTRIBUTION UPON WITHDRAWAL. Except as provided in this Article, upon withdrawal any withdrawing partner is entitled to receive any distribution to which he or she is entitled under the partnership agreement and, if not otherwise provided in the agreement, he or she is entitled to receive, within a reasonable time after withdrawal, the fair value of his or her interest in the limited partnership as of the date of withdrawal based upon his or her right to share in distributions from the limited partnership.

SECTION 605. DISTRIBUTION IN KIND. Except as provided in writing in the partnership agreement, a partner, regardless of the nature of his or her contribution, has no right to demand and receive any distribution from a limited partnership in any form other than cash. Except as provided in writing in the partnership agreement, a partner may not be compelled to accept a distribution of any asset in kind from a limited partnership to the extent that the percentage of the asset distributed to him or her exceeds a percentage of that asset which is equal to the percentage in which he or she shares in distributions from the limited partnership.

SECTION 606. RIGHT TO DISTRIBUTION. At the time a partner becomes entitled to receive a distribution, he or she has the status of, and is entitled to all remedies available to, a creditor of the limited partnership with respect to the distribution.

SECTION 607. LIMITATIONS ON DISTRIBUTION. A partner may not receive a distribution from a limited partnership to the extent that, after giving effect to the distribution, all liabilities of the limited partnership, other than liabilities to partners on account of their partnership interests, exceed the fair value of the partnership assets.

SECTION 608. LIABILITY UPON RETURN OF CONTRIBUTION. (a) If a partner has received the return of any part of his or her contribution without violation of the partnership agreement or this Act, he or she is liable to the limited partnership for a period of one year thereafter for the amount of the returned contribution, but only to the extent necessary to discharge the limited partnership's liabilities to creditors who extended credit to the limited partnership during the period the contribution was held by the partnership.

(b) If a partner has received the return of any part of his or her contribution in violation of the partnership agreement or this Act, he or she is liable to the limited partnership for a period of six years thereafter for the amount of the contribution wrongfully returned.

(c) A partner receives a return of his or her contribution to the extent that a distribution to him or her reduces his or her share of the fair value of the net assets of the limited partnership below the value, as set forth in the partnership records required to be kept pursuant to Section 105, of his contribution which has not been distributed to him or her.

ARTICLE 7

ASSIGNMENT OF PARTNERSHIP INTERESTS

SECTION 701. NATURE OF PARTNERSHIP INTEREST. A partnership interest is personal property.

SECTION 702. ASSIGNMENT OF PARTNERSHIP INTEREST. Except as provided in the partnership agreement, a partnership interest is assignable in whole or in part. An assignment of a partnership interest does not dissolve a limited partnership or entitle the assignee to become or to exercise any rights of a partner. An assignment entitles the assignee to receive, to the extent assigned, only the distribution to which the assignor would be entitled. Except as provided in the partnership agreement, a partner ceases to be a partner upon assignment of all his or her partnership interest.

SECTION 703. RIGHTS OF CREDITOR. On application to a court of competent jurisdiction by any judgment creditor of a partner, the court may charge the partnership interest of the partner with payment of the unsatisfied amount of the judgment with interest. To the extent so charged, the judgment creditor has only the rights of an assignee of the partnership interest. This Act does not deprive any partner of the benefit of any exemption laws applicable to his or her partnership interest.

SECTION 704. RIGHT OF ASSIGNEE TO BECOME LIMITED PARTNER.

(a) An assignee of a partnership interest, including an assignee of a general partner, may become a limited partner if and to the extent that

(i) the assignor gives the assignee that right in accordance with authority described in the partnership agreement, or

(ii) all other partners consent.

(b) An assignee who has become a limited partner has, to the extent assigned, the rights and powers, and is subject to the restrictions and liabilities, of a limited partner under the partnership agreement and this Act. An assignee who becomes a limited partner also is liable for the obligations of his or her assignor to make and return contributions as provided in Articles 5 and 6. However, the assignee is not obligated for liabilities unknown to the assignee at the time he or she became a limited partner.

(c) If an assignee of a partnership interest becomes a limited partner, the assignor is not released from his or her liability to the limited partnership under Sections 207 and 502.

SECTION 705. POWER OF ESTATE OF DECEASED OR INCOMPETENT PARTNER. If a partner who is an individual dies or a court of competent jurisdiction adjudges him or her to be incompetent to manage his or her person or his or her property, the partner's executor, administrator, guardian, conservator, or other legal representative may exercise all the partner's rights for the purpose of settling his or her estate or administering his or her property, including any power the partner had to give an assignee the right to become a limited partner. If a partner is a corporation, trust, or other entity and is dissolved or terminated, the powers of that partner may be exercised by its legal representative or successor.

ARTICLE 8

DISSOLUTION

SECTION 801. NONJUDICIAL DISSOLUTION. A limited partnership is dissolved and its affairs shall be wound up upon the happening of the first to occur of the following:

(1) at the time specified in the certificate of limited partnership;

(2) or upon the happening of events specified in writing in the partnership agreement;

(3) written consent of all partners;

(4) an event of withdrawal of a general partner unless at the time there is at least one other general partner and the written provisions of the partnership agreement permit the business of the limited partnership to be carried on by the remaining general partner and that partner does so, but the limited partnership is not dissolved and is not required to be wound up by reason of any event of withdrawal if, within 90 days after the withdrawal, all partners agree in writing to continue the business of the limited partnership and to the appointment of one or more additional general partners if necessary or desired; or

(5) entry of a decree of judicial dissolution under Section 802.

SECTION 802. JUDICIAL DISSOLUTION. On application by or for a partner the [designate the appropriate court] court may decree dissolution of a limited partnership whenever it is not reasonably practicable to carry on the business in conformity with the partnership agreement.

SECTION 803. WINDING UP. Except as provided in the partnership agreement, the general partners who have not wrongfully dissolved a limited partnership or, if none, the limited partners, may wind up the limited partnership's affairs; but the [designate the appropriate court] court may wind up the limited partnership's affairs upon application of any partner, his or her legal representative, or assignee.

SECTION 804. DISTRIBUTION OF ASSETS. Upon the winding up of a limited partnership, the assets shall be distributed as follows:

(1) to creditors, including partners who are creditors, to the extent permitted by law, in satisfaction of liabilities of the limited partnership other than liabilities for distributions to partners under Section 601 or 604;

(2) except as provided in the partnership agreement, to partners and former partners in satisfaction of liabilities for distributions under Section 601 or 604; and

(3) except as provided in the partnership agreement, to partners first for the return of their contributions and secondly respecting their partnership interests, in the proportions in which the partners share in distributions.

ARTICLE 9

FOREIGN LIMITED PARTNERSHIPS

SECTION 901. LAW GOVERNING. Subject to the Constitution of this State,

(i) the laws of the state under which a foreign limited partnership is organized govern its organization and internal affairs and the liability of its limited partners, and

(ii) a foreign limited partnership may not be denied registration by reason of any difference between those laws and the laws of this State.

SECTION 902. REGISTRATION. Before transacting business in this State, a foreign limited partnership shall register with the Secretary of State. In order to register, a foreign limited partnership shall submit to the Secretary of State, in duplicate, an application for registration as a foreign limited partnership, signed and sworn to by a general partner and setting forth:

(1) the name of the foreign limited partnership and, if different, the name under which it proposes to register and transact business in this State;

(2) the State and date of its formation;

(3) the name and address of any agent for service of process on the foreign limited partnership whom the foreign limited partnership elects to appoint; the agent must be an individual resident of this State, a domestic corporation, or a foreign corporation having a place of business in, and authorized to do business in, this State;

(4) a statement that the Secretary of State is appointed the agent of the foreign limited partnership for service of process if no agent has been appointed under paragraph (3) or, if appointed, the agent's authority has been revoked or if the agent cannot be found or served with the exercise of reasonable diligence;

(5) the address of the office required to be maintained in the state of its organization by the laws of that state or, if not so required, of the principal office of the foreign limited partnership;

(6) the name and business address of each general partner; and

(7) the address of the office at which is kept a list of the names and addresses of the limited partners and their capital contributions, together with an undertaking by the foreign limited partnership to keep those records until the foreign limited partnership's registration in this State is cancelled or withdrawn.

SECTION 903. ISSUANCE OF REGISTRATION.

(a) If the Secretary of State finds that an application for registration conforms to law and all requisite fees have been paid, he or she shall:

(1) endorse on the application the word "Filed," and the month, day and year of the filing thereof;

(2) file in his or her office a duplicate original of the application; and

(3) issue a certificate of registration to transact business in this State.(b) The certificate of registration, together with a duplicate original of the application, shall be returned to the person who filed the application or his or her representative.

SECTION 904. NAME. A foreign limited partnership may register with the Secretary of State under any name, whether or not it is the name under which it is registered in its state of organization, that includes without abbreviation the words "limited partnership" and that could be registered by a domestic limited partnership.

SECTION 905. CHANGES AND AMENDMENTS. If any statement in the application for registration of a foreign limited partnership was false when made or any arrangements or other facts described have changed, making the application inaccurate in any respect, the foreign limited partnership shall promptly file in the office of the Secretary of State a certificate, signed and sworn to by a general partner, correcting such statement.

SECTION 906. CANCELLATION OF REGISTRATION. A foreign limited partnership may cancel its registration by filing with the Secretary of State a certificate of cancellation signed and sworn to by a general partner. A cancellation does not terminate the authority of the Secretary of State to accept service of process on the foreign limited partnership with respect to [claims for relief] [causes of action] arising out of the transactions of business in this State.

SECTION 907. TRANSACTION OF BUSINESS WITHOUT REGISTRATION.(a) A foreign limited partnership transacting business in this State may not maintain any action, suit, or proceeding in any court of this State until it has registered in this State.

(b) The failure of a foreign limited partnership to register in this State does not impair the validity of any contract or act of the foreign limited partnership or prevent the foreign limited partnership from defending any action, suit, or proceeding in any court of this State.

(c) A limited partner of a foreign limited partnership is not liable as a general partner of the foreign limited partnership solely by reason of having transacted business in this State without registration.

(d) A foreign limited partnership, by transacting business in this State without registration, appoints the Secretary of State as its agent for service of process with respect to [claims for relief] [causes of action] arising out of the transaction of business in this State.

SECTION 908. ACTION BY [APPROPRIATE OFFICIAL]. The [designate the appropriate official] may bring an action to restrain a foreign limited partnership from transacting business in this State in violation of this Article.

ARTICLE 10

DERIVATIVE ACTIONS

SECTION 1001. RIGHT OF ACTION: A limited partner may bring an action in the right of a limited partnership to recover a judgment in its favor if general partners with authority to do so have refused to bring the action or if an effort to cause those general partners to bring the action is not likely to succeed.

SECTION 1002. PROPER PLAINTIFF. In a derivative action, the plaintiff must be a partner at the time of bringing the action and

(i) must have been a partner at the time of the transaction of which he or she complains or

(ii) his or her status as a partner must have devolved upon him or her by operation of law or pursuant to the terms of the partnership agreement from a person who was a partner at the time of the transaction.

SECTION 1003. PLEADING. In a derivative action, the complaint shall set forth with particularity the effort of the plaintiff to secure initiation of the action by a general partner or the reasons for not making the effort.

SECTION 1004. EXPENSES. If a derivative action is successful, in whole or in part, or if anything is received by the plaintiff as a result of a judgment, compromise or settlement of an action or claim, the court may award the plaintiff reasonable expenses, including reasonable attorney's fees, and shall direct him or her to remit to the limited partnership the remainder of those proceeds received by him or her.

ARTICLE 11

MISCELLANEOUS

SECTION 1101. CONSTRUCTION AND APPLICATION. This Act shall be so applied and construed to effectuate its general purpose to make uniform the law with respect to the subject of this Act among states enacting it.

SECTION 1102. SHORT TITLE. This Act may be cited as the Uniform Limited Partnership Act.

SECTION 1103. SEVERABILITY. If any provision of this Act or its application to any person or circumstance is held invalid, the invalidity does not affect other provisions or applications of the Act which can be given effect without the invalid provision or application, and to this end the provisions of this Act are severable.

SECTION 1104. EFFECTIVE DATE, EXTENDED EFFECTIVE DATE AND REPEAL. Except as set forth below, the effective date of this Act is __________ and the following acts [list existing limited partnership acts] are hereby repealed:

(1) The existing provisions for execution and filing of certificates of limited partnerships and amendments thereunder and cancellations thereof continue in effect until [specify time required to create central filing system], the extended effective date, and Sections 102, 103, 104, 105, 201, 202, 203, 204 and 206 are not effective until the extended effective date.

(2) Section 402, specifying the conditions under which a general partner ceases to be a member of a limited partnership, is not effective until the extended effective date, and the applicable provisions of existing law continue to govern until the extended effective date.

(3) Sections 501, 502 and 608 apply only to contributions and distributions made after the effective date of this Act.

(4) Section 704 applies only to assignments made after the effective date of this Act.

(5) Article 9, dealing with registration of foreign limited partnerships, is not effective until the extended effective date.

(6) Unless otherwise agreed by the partners, the applicable provisions of existing law governing allocation of profits and losses (rather than the provisions of Section 503), distributions to a withdrawing partner (rather than the provisions of Section 604), and distribution of assets upon the winding up of a limited partnership (rather than the provisions of Section 804) govern limited partnerships formed before the effective date of this Act.

SECTION 1105. RULES FOR CASES NOT PROVIDED FOR IN THIS ACT. In any case not provided for in this Act the provisions of the Uniform Partnership Act govern.

SECTION 1106. SAVINGS CLAUSE. The repeal of any statutory provision by this Act does not impair, or otherwise affect, the organization or the continued existence of a limited partnership existing at the effective date of this Act, nor does the repeal of any existing statutory provision by this Act impair any contract or affect any right accrued before the effective date of this Act.

Appendix E
Sample Filled-In Forms

These sample forms have been filled out for hypothetical Family Limited Partnerships in order to help you complete them for your new business. Refer to them when drafting the essential agreements and signing the required documents for your own Family Limited Partnership.

TRANSMITTAL LETTER

Secretary of State
(ADDRESS)

SUBJECT: Ruby's Slippers Ltd.
(Proposed family limited partnership name)

Enclosed are two (2) originals and one (1) copy of the Certificate of Limited Partnership and a check in the amount of $35.00 which represents the filing fee for a limited partnership.

Please return the enclosed photocopy to me with the filing date stamped on it.

FROM: Ruby Doe
Name (printed or typed)

123 Yellow Brick Rd
Street Address

Any City, OZ 01234
City, State & Zip Code

(555) 555-6789
Daytime telephone number

This page has been intentionally left blank.

Certificate of Assumed Name

The undersigned hereby certify the following:

1. The undersigned are conducting business as partners of a limited partnership under the laws of the State of Your State. The business conducted by the limited partnership is retail costume shop under the name of Frank's Costumes and it principal place of business is located at 123 Main Street, Any City.

2. The real names and residences of all of the partners of the limited partnership are:

General Partner: Frank N. Stein

Limited Partners: Suzie Stein
Jack L. Hyde

3. No other person is interested as a partner, part owner, or otherwise in the business or conduct of it.

This Certificate is executed and filed pursuant to state law relating to the conduct of business under a Fictitious/Assumed name.

SIGNED this 31st day of October, 2003.

Frank N. Stein
Partner

Suzie Stein
Partner

Jack L. Hyde
Partner

STATE OF Your State §
§
COUNTY OF Shelley §

On this 31st day of October, 2003, before me personally appeared Frank N. Stein, known to me to be the person whose name is subscribed to this Certificate and acknowledged to me that he/she executed the same in his/her authorized capacity as general partner of Frank's Costumes, and that by his/her signature on this Certificate the person or entity upon whose behalf the he/she acted, executed the Certificate.

____

Notary Public
State of ____________________________
My commission expires:_______________

STATE OF Your State §
§
COUNTY OF Shelley §

On this 31st day of October, 2003, before me personally appeared Suzie Stein, known to me to be the person whose name is subscribed to this Certificate and acknowledged to me that he/she executed the same in his/her authorized capacity as limited partner of Frank's Costumes, and that by his/her signature on this Certificate the person or entity upon whose behalf the he/she acted, executed the Certificate.

____

Notary Public
State of ____________________________
My commission expires:_______________

STATE OF Your State §
§
COUNTY OF Shelley §

On this 31st day of October, 2003, before me personally appeared Jack L. Hyde, known to me to be the person whose name is subscribed to this Certificate and acknowledged to me that he/she executed the same in his/her authorized capacity as limited partner of Frank's Costumes, and that by his/her signature on this Certificate the person or entity upon whose behalf the he/she acted, executed the Certificate.

____

Notary Public
State of ____________________________
My commission expires:_______________

Certificate of Limited Partnership

The partners of Frank's Costumes, Ltd.______________, a limited partnership formed under the laws of the State of Your State______, (hereinafter "Partnership"), hereby execute the following Certificate of Limited Partnership.

1. **Name of the Partnership**. The name of the Partnership is: Frank's Costumes, Ltd._______________.

2. **Registered Agent**. The registered agent for service of process for the Partnership is: Frank N. Stein_______________________.

3. **Registered Office**. The registered office of the Partnership is located at the following address 123 Main Street, Any City, Your State, 01234

4. **Name and address of General Partner**. The name(s) and address(es) of each general partner of the Partnership at the time of the original admission to the Partnership of such partner are the following:

GENERAL PARTNER	BUSINESS RESIDENCE OR MAILING ADDRESS
Frank N. Stein	123 Main Street Any City, Your State, 01234

5. **Partners**. There are at least two partners in the Partnership at least one of whom is a limited partner.

6. **Duration**. The Partnership shall continue for ten____ (_10_) years.

7. **Effective Date**. The Partnership shall be deemed formed on the date that this Certificate of Limited Partnership is filed in the office of the Secretary of State.

SIGNED this 31st____ day of October______, 20 03_____.

GENERAL PARTNER(S):

*Frank N. Stein*____________________ ____________________________

____________________________ ____________________________

This page has been intentionally left blank.

PARTNERSHIP AGREEMENT
OF
Frank's Costumes, Ltd
a Limited Partnership

The Partnership Agreement is made this 31st day of October, 2003, by and between Frank N. Stein, Suzie Stein, and Jack L. Hyde (individually the "Partner" and collectively the "Partners").

In consideration of the mutual terms, conditions and covenants hereinafter set forth, the Partners agree as follows:

I. GENERAL

1.1 The purpose of the Partnership shall be retail sales.

1.2 The name of the Partnership shall be Frank's Costumes, Ltd., (the "Partnership").

1.3 The Partnership shall be operated as a limited partnership under the laws of the State of Your State.

1.4 The initial address of the Partnership shall be 123 Main Street, Any City, which may be changed from time to time by the Partners.

1.5 The Partners shall execute the necessary documents to register the Partnership name and existence with the proper governmental offices in the County of Shelley, State of Your State.

1.6 The Partnership shall continue until, and dissolve upon, the first happening of:

a. The death of one Partner; or

b. The withdrawal, by written notice, of one Partner; or

c. The affirmative vote of a majority in interest of the Limited Partners.

II. CAPITALIZATION

2.1 The Partners shall contribute to the Partnership in the following amounts which shall reflect their Partnership interest:

Frank N. Stein	$ 5000	33 and 1/3 %
Suzie Stein	$5000	33 and 1/3 %
Jack L. Hyde	$5000	33 and 1/3 %
	$	%

2.2 No Partner shall receive interest on his capital contribution.

2.3 A separate "Capital Account" shall be maintained for each Partner.

a. A Capital Account shall be increased by (1) the contribution to the capital of the Partnership, including the initial contribution (Paragraph 2.1 above) and (2) the distributive share of the Net Profits of the Partnership; and decreased by (1) distributions, (2) the distributive share of Net Losses of the Partnership and (3) the distributive share of expenditures of the Partnership not deductible in computing Net Profits/Losses and not properly treated as capital expenditures.

b. Distributions in kind shall be valued at fair market value less any liability which the Partner assumes on the distribution or to which the asset distributed is subject.

2.4 If in the opinion of the majority in interest of the Limited Partners of the Partnership additional capital is needed for the proper conduct of the business of the Partnership, each Partner shall contribute pro rata in accordance with his interest.

2.5 No Limited Partner shall be liable for any obligation incurred by the General Partner on behalf of the Partnership. No Limited Partner shall be responsible for payment of any amount due a creditor of the Partnership.

III. MANAGEMENT

3.1 All matters to be determined by the Partners shall be determined by the affirmative vote of a majority in interest of the Limited Partners present at a meeting of the Partnership. All matters determined by the Partners shall be recorded in a Minute Book reflecting the date, matter discussed and the action taken.

3.2 The Partners shall meet at least once each year. Additional meetings may be held at the request of 66 2/3% of the Partnership by interest. All meetings shall be by written notice reasonably in advance of such meeting so that each Partner may be present either in person or by written proxy authorization.

3.3 At the first meeting of the Partnership to be held on November 1st, 2003, at 123 Main St., Any City, at 11 p.m./a.m., the Partnership shall determine:

a. the manner in which the business of the Partnership shall be managed;

b. the hiring of employees;

c. salaries to be paid to employees and the General Partner who participates in the day-to-day management of the business of the Partnership;

d. banking procedures; and

e. any other matters which may properly come before the Partnership.

3.4 The fiscal year of the Partnership shall end December 31.

3.5 Each Partner shall have the right to inspect the books, records, reports and accounts of the Partnership during normal business hours, which books, records, reports and accounts shall be kept at the Partnership's place of business or at such other place as determined from time to time by the Partnership.

IV. RESTRICTIONS

4.1 No Partner shall sell, assign, mortgage, hypothecate or encumber his interest in the Partnership without the express written permission of all the remaining Partners, without regard to interest.

4.2 All Partners shall meet their personal obligations and debts as they become due and each agrees to save and hold remaining Partners and the Partnership harmless from all costs, claims and demands with respect to such obligations and debts.

4.3 No Limited Partner shall:

a. lend any Partnership funds;

b incur any obligation in the name of or on the credit of the Partnership;

c. lend any of the Partner's funds to the Partnership, with or without interest;

d. sell, assign, mortgage, hypothecate or encumber any asset of the Partnership;

e. make an assignment of the assets of the Partnership for the benefit of creditors of the Partnership;

f. execute any guarantee on behalf of the Partnership;

g. release, assign or transfer a Partnership claim or any asset of the Partnership;

h. borrow in the name of the Partnership;

i. Submit any Partnership claim or liability in arbitration;

j. initiate, conduct or settle litigation in the name of or pertaining to the Partnership; or

k. invest Partnership funds or other assets.

4.4 Any Partner who commits a prohibited act shall be individually liable to the remaining Partners, pro rata to their Partnership interest, for any loss caused by the prohibited act.

V. PROFITS/LOSSES AND DISTRIBUTIONS

5.1 Net Profits/Losses shall be determined in accordance with good accounting principles and shall be as finally determined for federal income tax purposes.

5.2 Net Profits/Losses shall be apportioned pro rata among the Partners' capital account according to each Partner's interest.

5.3 Distribution shall be made upon the recommendation of the General Partner.

VI. ADDITIONAL PARTNERS/DISSOLUTION

6.1 The Partnership may admit additional Partners upon the affirmative vote of the Limited Partners, as provided herein. Additional Partners shall then be admitted upon payment of a contribution to capital as determined by the Partnership and each Partner's interest in the Partnership as provided for in paragraph 2.1 shall be redetermined.

6.2 In the event of the dissolution of the Partnership for any reason, the affairs of the Partnership shall be wound up and the proceeds of the Partnership distributed in accordance with the terms of this Agreement and the laws of the State of Your State____________.

VII. MISCELLANEOUS

7.1 If any controversy or claim arising out of this Agreement cannot be settled by the Partners, the controversy or claims shall be settled by arbitration in the City of Any City, State of Your State, in accordance with the rules of the American Arbitration Association then in effect, and judgment on the award my be entered in any court having jurisdiction.

7.2 This Agreement shall be enforced and construed under and shall be subject to the laws of the State of Your State. If any provision of this Agreement shall be unlawful, void or unenforceable, that provision shall be deemed separate from and in no way shall affect the validity or enforceability of the remaining provisions of this Agreement.

7.3 All notices required to be given under this Agreement shall be either (1) personally delivered to the party to whom addressed or (2) sent by U.S. Mail, postage prepaid, Certified mail, Return Receipt Requested, addressed to the Partner at the last address for that Partner as maintained by the Partnership.

7.4 This Agreement contains the full and complete understanding of all of the Partners with reference to the Partnership and supercedes all prior agreements and understandings, whether written or oral. This Agreement may not be amended except in writing and upon the consent of all of the Partners then existing of the Partnership.

7.5 This Agreement shall be binding on and inure to the benefit of the respective successors, permitted assigns, executors, administrators, personal representatives and beneficiaries of the Partners.

EXECUTED by the Partners as of the date first above written.

Frank N. Stein

General Partner

Suzie Stein

Limited Partner

Jack L. Hyde

Limited Partner

This page has been intentionally left blank.

Sale of Partnership Interest to Partners

Date: October 31, 2003

TO: Frank N. Stein

Jack L. Hyde

____

Partners:

In consideration of the sum of $10,000 to be paid by me upon the execution of this Agreement of Sale of a Partnership Interest, we agree as follows:

1. I hereby sell and transfer my entire interest as a partner in Frank's Costumes, Ltd., a limited partnership organized under the laws of the State of Your State ("Partnership") to be divided among you as you may determine.

2. Have no objection to, and grant you the right to continue to do business under the partnership name of Frank's Costumes, Ltd..

3. It is understood that I shall have the right to engage in a business similar to that engaged in by the Partnership and that nothing contained herein shall be deemed a covenant on my part not to compete.

4. There shall be a public announcement communicated to all those with whom the Partnership has done business in the past that I am no longer a member of the Partnership.

5. Each of us hereby releases the other from all past and present claims or obligations whatsoever as between the Partnership, each of you, and myself.

IN WITNESS WHEREOF the parties have signed this Agreement.

Frank N. Stein
General Partner

Suzie Stein
Limited Partner

Jack L. Hyde
Limited Partner

This page has been intentionally left blank.

GENERAL ASSIGNMENT

BE IT KNOWN, for value received, the undersigned Suzie Stein ____________, of Frank's Costumes, Ltd. hereby unconditionally and irrevocably assigns and transfers unto Frank's Costumes, Ltd. , a limited partnership formed and operated under the laws of the State of Your State ____________, all right, title and interest to the following property:

All Ms. Stein's 33 1/3% of partnership assets, equaling a value of $5,000.

The undersigned fully warrants that it has full rights and authority to enter into this assignment and that the rights and benefits hereunder assigned are free and clear of any lien, encumbrance, adverse claim or interest by any third party.

This assignment shall be binding upon and inure to the benefit of the parties, and their successors and assigns.

SIGNED this 31st ______ day of October ________________, 20 03 .

Jack L. Hyde ________________
Witness

Suzie Stein ________________
Assignor

GENERAL PARTNER OF
LIMITED PARTNERSHIP:

Frank N. Stein ________________
Witness

Frank N. Stein ________________

This page has been intentionally left blank.

QUITCLAIM DEED

THIS QUITCLAIM DEED, executed this 7th day of August, 20 03, by Toto Gale, the Grantor, whose post office address is: 222 Tornado Alley, Anywhere, Oz to Ruby's Slippers, Ltd., the Grantee, a limited partnership organized under the laws of the State of Oz, whose post office address is: 123 Yellow Brick Road, Any City, Oz, 01234.

WITNESSETH, that the Grantor, for good consideration and for the sum of Seven thousand Dollars ($ 7,000) paid by the Grantee, the receipt of which is hereby acknowledged, does hereby transfer, release and quitclaim to Grantee, forever, all right, title, interest and claim which the Grantor has in and to the following described parcel of land, and improvements and appurtenances thereto in the County of Emerald, State of Oz, to wit:

Toto's Farm (10 acres)

IN WITNESS WHEREOF, the Grantor has signed and sealed these presents the day and year first above written. Signed, sealed and delivered in the presence of:

Ruby Doe	*Toto Gale*
Witness	Grantor
Anne T. Em	
Witness	

STATE OF Oz________________ §
§
COUNTY OF Emerald____________ §

On this 7th__ day of August__________, 20 03____, before me personally appeared Toto Gale__________________, known to me to be the person whose name is subscribed to this Quitclaim Deed and acknowledged to me that he/she executed the same in his/her authorized capacity and that by his/her signature on this Quitclaim Deed the person or entity upon whose behalf the he/she acted, executed the Quitclaim Deed.

____
Notary Public
State of ___________________________
My commission expires:_____________

STATE OF Oz________________ §
§
COUNTY OF Emerald____________ §

On this 7th___ day of August__________, 20 03_____, before me personally appeared Ruby Doe__________________, known to me to be the person whose name is subscribed to this Quitclaim Deed and acknowledged to me that he/she executed the same in his/her authorized capacity and that by his/her signature on this Quitclaim Deed the person or entity upon whose behalf the he/she acted, executed the Quitclaim Deed.

____
Notary Public
State of ___________________________
My commission expires:_____________

SALE OF PARTNERSHIP INTEREST

AGREEMENT made this 16th day of September, 20 03 , by and between Anne T. Em , ______________, and Belinda Goodwich .

Anne T. Em is a General/Limited Partner in the limited partnership named Ruby's Slippers, Ltd. , a limited partnership organized under the laws of the State of Oz (the "Partnership"). Pursuant to a Partnership Agreement dated July 22 , 20 03 .

Pursuant to the Partnership Agreement, Anne T. Em has obtained the approval of the remaining partners to the sale of his/her entire interest in the Partnership.

IT IS THEREFORE AGREED:

1. Anne T. Em hereby sells and transfers his/her entire partnership interest in the Partnership to Belinda Goodwich for the sum of $ 15,000 payable upon the execution of this Agreement receipt of which is hereby acknowledged.

2. Belinda Goodwich agrees to be bound by the terms of the Partnership Agreement dated July 22 , 20 03 , as if he/she had been originally named therein.

IN WITNESS WHEREOF the parties have signed this Agreement on the date first above-written.

Anne T. Em
Selling Partner

Belinda Goodwich
Purchaser

APPROVED:

Ruby Doe General Partner	______________ Limited Partner
Dorothy Doe Limited Partner	______________ Limited Partner

This page has been intentionally left blank.

CHANGE OF REGISTERED AGENT/REGISTERED OFFICE

1. The name of the limited partnership is Frank's Costumes, Ltd. and the file number issued to the limited partnership by the Secretary of State is 12-3456.

2. The changes set forth herein are authorized under the laws of the State of Your State.

3. The registered office of the limited partnership presently shown in the records of the Secretary of State is 123 Main Street, Any City, Your State.

_____ A. The address of the NEW registered office is :__________________

or

__X__ B. The registered office address will not change

4. The name of the registered agent as presently shown in the records of the Secretary of State is Frank N. Stein.

__X__ A. The name of the NEW registered agent is Jack L. Hyde.

or

_____ B. The registered agent will not change.

By: *Frank N. Stein*
General Partner

This page has been intentionally left blank.

CERTIFICATE OF WITHDRAWAL

The following is hereby certified:

1. The undersigned, Suzie Stein, whose address is 119 Tranxylvanis Ave., Any City, has withdrawn as a limited/general partner from the partnership doing business under the laws of the State of Your State under the name of Frank's Costumes, Ltd..

2. The partnership has its principal place of business located at: 123 Main Street, Any City, Shelly, County, State of Your State.

3. The Assumed/Fictitious name Certificate with respect to the business name was filed in the office of Any City, State of Your State, on the 31st day of October, 2003.

Signed this 20th day of October, 20 04.

ACCEPTED BY:

Frank N. Stein	*Suzie Stein*
General Partner	Withdrawing Partner

STATE OF Your State §
§
COUNTY OF Shelley §

On this 20th day of December, 2004, before me personally appeared Frank N. Stein, known to me to be the person whose name is subscribed to this Certificate and acknowledged to me that he/she executed the same in his/her authorized capacity as general partner of Frank's Costumes, Ltd.__________, and that by his/her signature on this Certificate the person or entity upon whose behalf the he/she acted, executed the Certificate.

____

Notary Public
State of ___________________________
My commission expires:______________

STATE OF Your State______________ §
§
COUNTY OF Shelley______________ §

On this 20th__ day of December__________, 2004____, before me personally appeared Suzie Stein__________________, known to me to be the person whose name is subscribed to this Certificate and acknowledged to me that he/she executed the same in his/her authorized capacity as limited partner of Frank's Costumes, Ltd.__________, and that by his/her signature on this Certificate the person or entity upon whose behalf the he/she acted, executed the Certificate.

____

Notary Public
State of ___________________________
My commission expires:______________

Form **SS-4**
(Rev. April 2000)
Department of the Treasury
Internal Revenue Service

Application for Employer Identification Number

(For use by employers, corporations, partnerships, trusts, estates, churches, government agencies, certain individuals, and others. See instructions.)

► Keep a copy for your records.

EIN

OMB No. 1545-0003

Please type or print clearly.

1 Name of applicant (legal name) (see instructions)
Sidney Bones

2 Trade name of business (if different from name on line 1)
Bones Enterprises

3 Executor, trustee, "care of" name
Sidney Bones

4a Mailing address (street address) (room, apt., or suite no.)
6789 Graves Avenue

5a Business address (if different from address on lines 4a and 4b)

4b City, state, and ZIP code
Chicago, Il 60601

5b City, state, and ZIP code

6 County and state where principal business is located
Cook, IL

7 Name of principal officer, general partner, grantor, owner, or trustor—SSN or ITIN may be required (see instructions) ►
Sidney Bones 123-45-6789

8a Type of entity (Check only one box.) (see instructions)
Caution: *If applicant is a limited liability company, see the instructions for line 8a.*

- ☐ Sole proprietor (SSN) ______
- ☒ Partnership
- ☐ Personal service corp.
- ☐ REMIC
- ☐ National Guard
- ☐ State/local government
- ☐ Farmers' cooperative
- ☐ Church or church-controlled organization
- ☐ Other nonprofit organization (specify) ► ______ (enter GEN if applicable) ______
- ☐ Other (specify) ►
- ☐ Estate (SSN of decedent) ______
- ☐ Plan administrator (SSN) ______
- ☐ Other corporation (specify) ► ______
- ☐ Trust
- ☐ Federal government/military

8b If a corporation, name the state or foreign country (if applicable) where incorporated | State | Foreign country

9 Reason for applying (Check only one box.) (see instructions)
- ☒ Started new business (specify type) ► novelty store
- ☐ Hired employees (Check the box and see line 12.)
- ☐ Created a pension plan (specify type) ►
- ☐ Banking purpose (specify purpose) ►
- ☐ Changed type of organization (specify new type) ►
- ☐ Purchased going business
- ☐ Created a trust (specify type) ►
- ☐ Other (specify) ►

10 Date business started or acquired (month, day, year) (see instructions)
01-29-02

11 Closing month of accounting year (see instructions)
December

12 First date wages or annuities were paid or will be paid (month, day, year). **Note:** *If applicant is a withholding agent, enter date income will first be paid to nonresident alien. (month, day, year)* . . . . ► 02-13-02

13 Highest number of employees expected in the next 12 months. **Note:** *If the applicant does not expect to have any employees during the period, enter -0-. (see instructions)* . . . . ►

Nonagricultural	Agricultural	Household
3	0	0

14 Principal activity (see instructions) ► novelty sales

15 Is the principal business activity manufacturing? . . . . ☐ **Yes** ☒ **No**
If "Yes," principal product and raw material used ►

16 To whom are most of the products or services sold? Please check one box.
☐ Business (wholesale)
☒ Public (retail) ☐ Other (specify) ► ☐ N/A

17a Has the applicant ever applied for an employer identification number for this or any other business? . . . . . ☐ **Yes** ☒ **No**
Note: *If "Yes," please complete lines 17b and 17c.*

17b If you checked "Yes" on line 17a, give applicant's legal name and trade name shown on prior application, if different from line 1 or 2 above.
Legal name ► Trade name ►

17c Approximate date when and city and state where the application was filed. Enter previous employer identification number if known.

Approximate date when filed (mo., day, year)	City and state where filed	Previous EIN

Under penalties of perjury, I declare that I have examined this application, and to the best of my knowledge and belief, it is true, correct, and complete.

Business telephone number (include area code) (630) 555-0000

Fax telephone number (include area code) (630) 555-0001

Name and title (Please type or print clearly.) ► Sidney Bones, owner

Signature ► *Sidney Bones* Date ► *01/29/03*

Note: *Do not write below this line. For official use only.*

Please leave blank ►	Geo.	Ind.	Class	Size	Reason for applying

For Privacy Act and Paperwork Reduction Act Notice, see page 4. Cat. No. 16055N Form **SS-4** (Rev. 4-2000)

Do I Need an EIN?

File Form SS-4 if the applicant entity does not already have an EIN but is required to show an EIN on a return, statement, or other document.[1] **See also the separate instructions for each line on Form SS-4**

IF the applicant...	AND...	THEN...
Started a new business	Does not currently have (nor expect to have) employees	Complete lines 1, 2, 4a-6, 8a, and
Hired (or will hire) employees, including household employees	Does not already have an EIN	Complete lines 1, 2, 4a-6, 7a-b (if 8a, 8b (if applicable), and 9-16c.
Opened a bank account	Needs an EIN for banking purposes only	Complete lines 1-5b, 7a-b (if appli 9, and 16a-c.
Changed type of organization	Either the legal character of the organization or its ownership changed (e.g., you incorporate a sole proprietorship or form a partnership)[2]	Complete lines 1-16c (as applicabl
Purchased a going business[3]	Does not already have an EIN	Complete lines 1-16c (as applicabl
Created a trust	The trust is other than a grantor trust or an IRA trust[4]	Complete lines 1-16c (as applicabl
Created a pension plan as a plan administrator[5]	Needs an EIN for reporting purposes	Complete lines 1, 2, 4a-6, 8a, 9, a
Is a foreign person needing an EIN to comply with IRS withholding regulations	Needs an EIN to complete a Form W-8 (other than Form W-8ECI), avoid withholding on portfolio assets, or claim tax treaty benefits[6]	Complete lines 1-5b, 7a-b (SSN or optional), 8a-9, and 16a-c.
Is administering an estate	Needs an EIN to report estate income on Form 1041	Complete lines 1, 3, 4a-b, 8a, 9, a
Is a withholding agent for taxes on non-wage income paid to an alien (i.e., individual, corporation, or partnership, etc.)	Is an agent, broker, fiduciary, manager, tenant, or spouse who is required to file **Form 1042,** Annual Withholding Tax Return for U.S. Source Income of Foreign Persons	Complete lines 1, 2, 3 (if applicable 7a-b (if applicable), 8a, 9, and 16a-
Is a state or local agency	Serves as a tax reporting agent for public assistance recipients under Rev. Proc. 80-4, 1980-1 C.B. 581[7]	Complete lines 1, 2, 4a-5b, 8a, 9,
Is a single-member LLC	Needs an EIN to file **Form 8832,** Classification Election, for filing employment tax returns, **or** for state reporting purposes[8]	Complete lines 1-16c (as applicabl
Is an S corporation	Needs an EIN to file **Form 2553,** Election by a Small Business Corporation[9]	Complete lines 1-16c (631-447-4955 bl

[1] For example, a sole proprietorship or self-employed farmer who establishes a qualified retirement plan, or is required to file excise, employment, al or firearms returns, must have an EIN. **A partnership, corporation, REMIC (real estate mortgage investment conduit), nonprofit organization (etc.), or farmers' cooperative must use an EIN for any tax-related purpose even if the entity does not have employees.**

[2] However, **do not** apply for a new EIN if the existing entity only **(a)** changed its business name, **(b)** elected on Form 8832 to change the way it is ta covered by the default rules), or **(c)** terminated its partnership status because at least 50% of the total interests in partnership capit 816-823-7777 w exchanged within a 12-month period. (The EIN of the terminated partnership should continue to be used. See Regulations section 301.6109-1(d)(2)

[3] Do not use the EIN of the prior business unless you became the "owner" of a corporation by acquiring its stock.

[4] However, IRA trusts that are required to file **Form 990-T,** Exempt Organization Business Income Tax Return, must have an EIN.

[5] A plan administrator is the person or group of persons specified as the administrator by the instrument under which the plan is operated.

[6] Entities applying to be a Qualified Intermediary (QI) need a QI-EIN even if they already have an EIN. **See Rev. Proc. 2000-12.**

[7] See also *Household employer* on page 4. (**Note:** State or local agencies may need an EIN for other reasons, e.g., hired employees.)

Kansas, New Mexico, Oklahoma, Texas	Attn: Entity Control Austin, TX 73301 512-460-7843
Alaska, Arizona, California (counties of Alpine, Amador, Butte, Calaveras, Colusa, Contra Costa, Del Norte, El Dorado, Glenn, Humboldt, Lake, Lassen, Marin, Mendocino, Modoc, Napa, Nevada, Placer, Plumas, Sacramento, San Joaquin, Shasta, Sierra, Siskiyou, Solano, Sonoma, Sutter, Tehama, Trinity, Yolo, and Yuba), Colorado, Idaho, Montana, Nebraska, Nevada, North Dakota, Oregon, South Dakota, Utah, Washington, Wyoming	Attn: Entity Control Mail Stop 6271 P.O. Box 9941 Ogden, UT 84201 801-620-7645
California (all other counties), Hawaii	Attn: Entity Control Fresno, CA 93888 559-452-4010
Alabama, Arkansas, Louisiana, Mississippi, North Carolina, Tennessee	Attn: Entity Control Memphis, TN 37501 901-546-3920
If you have no legal residence, principal place of business, or principal office or agency in any state	Attn: Entity Control Philadelphia, PA 19255 215-516-6999

Specific Instructions

The instructions that follow are for those items that are not self-explanatory. Enter N/A (nonapplicable) on the lines that do not apply.

Line 1. Enter the legal name of the entity applying for the EIN exactly as it appears on the social security card, charter, or other applicable legal document.

Individuals. Enter your first name, middle initial, and last name. If you are a sole proprietor, enter your individual name, not your business name. Enter your business name on line 2. Do not use abbreviations or nicknames on line 1.

Trusts. Enter the name of the trust.

Estate of a decedent. Enter the name of the estate.

Partnerships. Enter the legal name of the partnership as it appears in the partnership agreement. **Do not** list the names of the partners on line 1. See the specific instructions for line 7.

Corporations. Enter the corporate name as it appears in the corporation charter or other legal document creating it.

Plan administrators. Enter the name of the plan administrator. A plan administrator who already has an EIN should use that number.

Line 2. Enter the trade name of the business if different from the legal name. The trade name is the "doing business as" name.

Note: *Use the full legal name on line 1 on all tax returns filed for the entity. However, if you enter a trade name on line 2 and choose to use the trade name instead of the legal name, enter the trade name on all returns you file. To prevent processing delays and errors,* ***always*** *use either the legal name only or the trade name only on all tax returns.*

Line 3. Trusts enter the name of the trustee. Estates enter the name of the executor, administrator, or other fiduciary. If the entity applying has a designated person to receive tax information, enter that person's name as the "care of" person. Print or type the first name, middle initial, and last name.

Line 7. Enter the first name, middle initial, last name, and SSN of a principal officer if the business is a corporation; of a general partner if a partnership; of the owner of a single member entity that is disregarded as an entity separate from its owner; or of a grantor, owner, or trustor if a trust. If the person in question is an alien individual with a previously assigned individual taxpayer identification number (ITIN), enter the ITIN in the space provided, instead of an SSN. You are not required to enter an SSN or ITIN if the reason you are applying for an EIN is to make an entity classification election (see Regulations section 301.7701-1 through 301.7701-3), and you are a nonresident alien with no effectively connected income from sources within the United States.

Line 8a. Check the box that best describes the type of entity applying for the EIN. If you are an alien individual with an ITIN previously assigned to you, enter the ITIN in place of a requested SSN.

Caution: *This is not an election for a tax classification of an entity. See "Limited liability company (LLC)" below.*

If not specifically mentioned, check the "Other" box, enter the type of entity and the type of return that will be filed (for example, common trust fund, Form 1065). Do not enter N/A. If you are an alien individual applying for an EIN, see the **Line 7** instructions above.

Sole proprietor. Check this box if you file Schedule C, C-EZ, or F (Form 1040) and have a qualified plan, or are required to file excise, employment, or alcohol, tobacco, or firearms returns, or are a payer of gambling winnings. Enter your SSN (or ITIN) in the space provided. If you are a nonresident alien with are a nonresident alien with no effectively connected income from sources within the United States, you do not need to enter an SSN or ITIN.

REMIC. Check this box if the entity has elected to be treated as a real estate mortgage investment conduit (REMIC). See the Instructions for Form 1066 for more information.

Other nonprofit organization. Check this box if the nonprofit organization is other than a church or church-controlled organization and specify the type of nonprofit organization (for example, an educational organization).

If the organization also seeks tax-exempt status, you must file either **Package 1023,** Application for Recognition of Exemption, or **Package 1024,** Application for Recognition of Exemption Under Section 501(a). Get **Pub. 557,** Tax Exempt Status for Your Organization, for more information.

Group exemption number (GEN). If the organization is covered by a group exemption letter, enter the four-digit GEN. (Do not confuse the GEN with the nine-digit EIN.) If you do not know the GEN, contact the parent organization. Get Pub. 557 for more information about group exemption numbers.

Withholding agent. If you are a withholding agent required to file Form 1042, check the "Other" box and enter "Withholding agent."

Personal service corporation. Check this box if the entity is a personal service corporation. An entity is a personal service corporation for a tax year only if:

- The principal activity of the entity during the testing period (prior tax year) for the tax year is the performance of personal services substantially by employee-owners, and
- The employee-owners own at least 10% of the fair market value of the outstanding stock in the entity on the last day of the testing period.

Personal services include performance of services in such fields as health, law, accounting, or consulting. For more information about personal service corporations, see the **Instructions for Forms 1120 and 1120-A,** and **Pub. 542,** Corporations.

Limited liability company (LLC). See the definition of limited liability company in the **Instructions for Form 1065,** U.S. Partnership Return of Income. An LLC with two or more members can be a partnership or an association taxable as a corporation. An LLC with a single owner can be an association taxable as a corporation or an entity disregarded as an entity separate from its owner. See Form 8832 for more details.

Note: *A domestic LLC with at least two members that does not file Form 8832 is classified as a partnership for Federal income tax purposes.*

- If the entity is classified as a partnership for Federal income tax purposes, check the "partnership" box.
- If the entity is classified as a corporation for Federal income tax purposes, check the "Other corporation" box and write "limited liability co." in the space provided.
- If the entity is disregarded as an entity separate from its owner, check the "Other" box and write in "disregarded entity" in the space provided.

Plan administrator. If the plan administrator is an individual, enter the plan administrator's SSN in the space provided.

Other corporation. This box is for any corporation other than a personal service corporation. If you check this box, enter the type of corporation (such as insurance company) in the space provided.

Household employer. If you are an individual, check the "Other" box and enter "Household employer" and your SSN. If you are a state or local agency serving as a tax reporting agent for public assistance recipients who become household employers, check the "Other" box and enter "Household employer agent." If you are a trust that qualifies as a household employer, you do not need a separate EIN for reporting tax information relating to household employees; use the EIN of the trust.

QSub. For a qualified subchapter S subsidiary (QSub) check the "Other" box and specify "QSub."

Line 9. Check only **one** box. Do not enter N/A.

Started new business. Check this box if you are starting a new business that requires an EIN. If you check this box, enter the type of business being started. **Do not** apply if you already have an EIN and are only adding another place of business.

Hired employees. Check this box if the existing business is requesting an EIN because it has hired or is hiring employees and is therefore required to file employment tax returns. **Do not** apply if you already have an EIN and are only hiring employees. For information on the applicable employment taxes for family members, see **Circular E,** Employer's Tax Guide (Publication 15).

Created a pension plan. Check this box if you have created a pension plan and need an EIN for reporting purposes. Also, enter the type of plan.

Note: *Check this box if you are applying for a trust EIN when a new pension plan is established.*

Banking purpose. Check this box if you are requesting an EIN for banking purposes only, and enter the banking purpose (for example, a bowling league for depositing dues or an investment club for dividend and interest reporting).

Changed type of organization. Check this box if the business is changing its type of organization, for example, if the business was a sole proprietorship and has been incorporated or has become a partnership. If you check this box, specify in the space provided the type of change made, for example, "from sole proprietorship to partnership."

Purchased going business. Check this box if you purchased an existing business. **Do not** use the former owner's EIN. **Do not** apply for a new EIN if you already have one. Use your own EIN.

Created a trust. Check this box if you created a trust, and enter the type of trust created. For example, indicate if the trust is a nonexempt charitable trust or a split-interest trust.

Note: *Do not check this box if you are applying for a trust EIN when a new pension plan is established. Check "Created a pension plan."*

Exception. Do **not** file this form for certain grantor-type trusts. The trustee does not need an EIN for the trust if the trustee furnishes the name and TIN of the grantor/owner and the address of the trust to all payors. See the Instructions for Form 1041 for more information.

Other (specify). Check this box if you are requesting an EIN for any other reason, and enter the reason.

Line 10. If you are starting a new business, enter the starting date of the business. If the business you acquired is already operating, enter the date you acquired the business. Trusts should enter the date the trust was legally created. Estates should enter the date of death of the decedent whose name appears on line 1 or the date when the estate was legally funded.

Line 11. Enter the last month of your accounting year or tax year. An accounting or tax year is usually 12 consecutive months, either a calendar year or a fiscal year (including a period of 52 or 53 weeks). A calendar year is 12 consecutive months ending on December 31. A fiscal year is either 12 consecutive months ending on the last day of any month other than December or a 52-53 week year. For more information on accounting periods, see **Pub. 538,** Accounting Periods and Methods.

Individuals. Your tax year generally will be a calendar year.

Partnerships. Partnerships generally must adopt one of the following tax years:

- The tax year of the majority of its partners,
- The tax year common to all of its principal partners,
- The tax year that results in the least aggregate deferral of income, or
- In certain cases, some other tax year.

See the Instructions for Form 1065 for more information.

REMIC. REMICs must have a calendar year as their tax year.

Personal service corporations. A personal service corporation generally must adopt a calendar year unless:

- It can establish a business purpose for having a different tax year, or
- It elects under section 444 to have a tax year other than a calendar year.

Trusts. Generally, a trust must adopt a calendar year except for the following:

- Tax-exempt trusts,
- Charitable trusts, and
- Grantor-owned trusts.

Line 12. If the business has or will have employees, enter the date on which the business began or will begin to pay wages. If the business does not plan to have employees, enter N/A.

Withholding agent. Enter the date you began or will begin to pay income to a nonresident alien. This also applies to individuals who are required to file Form 1042 to report alimony paid to a nonresident alien.

Line 13. For a definition of agricultural labor (farmwork), see **Circular A,** Agricultural Employer's Tax Guide (Publication 51).

Line 14. Generally, enter the exact type of business being operated (for example, advertising agency, farm, food or beverage establishment, labor union, real estate agency, steam laundry, rental of coin-operated vending machine, or investment club). Also state if the business will involve the sale or distribution of alcoholic beverages.

Governmental. Enter the type of organization (state, county, school district, municipality, etc.).

Nonprofit organization (other than governmental). Enter whether organized for religious, educational, or humane purposes, and the principal activity (for example, religious organization—hospital, charitable).

Mining and quarrying. Specify the process and the principal product (for example, mining bituminous coal, contract drilling for oil, or quarrying dimension stone).

Contract construction. Specify whether general contracting or special trade contracting. Also, show the type of work normally performed (for example, general contractor for residential buildings or electrical subcontractor).

Food or beverage establishments. Specify the type of establishment and state whether you employ workers who receive tips (for example, lounge—yes).

Trade. Specify the type of sales and the principal line of goods sold (for example, wholesale dairy products, manufacturer's representative for mining machinery, or retail hardware).

Manufacturing. Specify the type of establishment operated (for example, sawmill or vegetable cannery).

Signature. The application must be signed by (a) the individual, if the applicant is an individual, (b) the president, vice president, or other principal officer, if the applicant is a corporation, (c) a responsible and duly authorized member or officer having knowledge of its affairs, if the applicant is a partnership or other unincorporated organization, or (d) the fiduciary, if the applicant is a trust or an estate.

How To Get Forms and Publications

Phone. You can order forms, instructions, and publications by phone 24 hours a day, 7 days a week. Just call 1-800-TAX-FORM (1-800-829-3676). You should receive your order or notification of its status within 10 workdays.

Personal computer. With your personal computer and modem, you can get the forms and information you need using IRS's Internet Web Site at **www.irs.gov** or File Transfer Protocol at **ftp.irs.gov.**

CD-ROM. For small businesses, return preparers, or others who may frequently need tax forms or publications, a CD-ROM containing over 2,000 tax products (including many prior year forms) can be purchased from the National Technical Information Service (NTIS).

To order **Pub. 1796,** Federal Tax Products on CD-ROM, call **1-877-CDFORMS** (1-877-233-6767) toll free or connect to **www.irs.gov/cdorders**

Privacy Act and Paperwork Reduction Act Notice. We ask for the information on this form to carry out the Internal Revenue laws of the United States. We need it to comply with section 6109 and the regulations thereunder which generally require the inclusion of an employer identification number (EIN) on certain returns, statements, or other documents filed with the Internal Revenue Service. Information on this form may be used to determine which Federal tax returns you are required to file and to provide you with related forms and publications. We disclose this form to the Social Security Administration for their use in determining compliance with applicable laws. We will be unable to issue an EIN to you unless you provide all of the requested information which applies to your entity.

You are not required to provide the information requested on a form that is subject to the Paperwork Reduction Act unless the form displays a valid OMB control number. Books or records relating to a form or its instructions must be retained as long as their contents may become material in the administration of any Internal Revenue law. Generally, tax returns/return information are confidential, as required by section 6103.

The time needed to complete and file this form will vary depending on individual circumstances. The estimated average time is:

Recordkeeping	7 min.
Learning about the law or the form	22 min.
Preparing the form	46 min.
Copying, assembling, and sending the form to the IRS	20 min.

If you have comments concerning the accuracy of these time estimates or suggestions for making this form simpler, we would be happy to hear from you. You can write to the Tax Forms Committee, Western Area Distribution Center, Rancho Cordova, CA 95743-0001. **Do not** send the form to this address. Instead, see **Where To Apply** on page 2.

Form **1065**
Department of the Treasury
Internal Revenue Service

U.S. Return of Partnership Income

For calendar year 2001, or tax year beginning 1-01- , 2001, and ending 12-31 20 01
▶ See separate instructions.

OMB No. 1545-0099
2001

A Principal business activity: retail sales
B Principal product or service: slippers
C Business code number: 123456

Use the IRS label. Otherwise, print or type.

Name of partnership: Ruby's Slippers, Ltd.
Number, street, and room or suite no. If a P.O. box, see page 13 of the instructions.: 123 Yellow Brick Road
City or town, state, and ZIP code: Any City, OZ 01234

D Employer identification number: 00 0000012
E Date business started: 1-01-00
F Total assets (see page 14 of the instructions) $

G Check applicable boxes: (1) ☐ Initial return (2) ☒ Final return (3) ☐ Name change (4) ☐ Address change (5) ☐ Amended return
H Check accounting method: (1) ☐ Cash (2) ☒ Accrual (3) ☐ Other (specify) ▶
I Number of Schedules K-1. Attach one for each person who was a partner at any time during the tax year ▶ 4

Caution: *Include **only** trade or business income and expenses on lines 1a through 22 below. See the instructions for more information.*

Section	Line	Description	Sub-line	Sub-amount	Line	Amount
Income	1a	Gross receipts or sales	1a	404,037		
	b	Less returns and allowances	1b	3,114	1c	400,923
	2	Cost of goods sold (Schedule A, line 8)			2	255,760
	3	Gross profit. Subtract line 2 from line 1c			3	145,163
	4	Ordinary income (loss) from other partnerships, estates, and trusts *(attach schedule)*			4	
	5	Net farm profit (loss) *(attach Schedule F (Form 1040))*			5	
	6	Net gain (loss) from Form 4797, Part II, line 18			6	
	7	Other income (loss) *(attach schedule)*			7	
	8	**Total income (loss).** Combine lines 3 through 7			8	145,163
Deductions (see page 15 of the instructions for limitations)	9	Salaries and wages (other than to partners) (less employment credits)			9	30,172
	10	Guaranteed payments to partners			10	25,000
	11	Repairs and maintenance			11	1225
	12	Bad debts			12	215
	13	Rent			13	20,000
	14	Taxes and licenses			14	3,110
	15	Interest			15	1,326
	16a	Depreciation (if required, attach Form 4562)	16a			
	b	Less depreciation reported on Schedule A and elsewhere on return	16b		16c	
	17	Depletion **(Do not deduct oil and gas depletion.)**			17	
	18	Retirement plans, etc.			18	
	19	Employee benefit programs			19	
	20	Other deductions *(attach schedule)*			20	2806
	21	**Total deductions.** Add the amounts shown in the far right column for lines 9 through 20			21	84,394
	22	**Ordinary income (loss)** from trade or business activities. Subtract line 21 from line 8			22	60,769

Sign Here

Under penalties of perjury, I declare that I have examined this return, including accompanying schedules and statements, and to the best of my knowledge and belief, it is true, correct, and complete. Declaration of preparer (other than general partner or limited liability company member) is based on all information of which preparer has any knowledge.

Ruby Doe — Signature of general partner or limited liability company member
4/3/02 — Date

May the IRS discuss this return with the preparer shown below (see instructions)? ☐ Yes ☐ No

Paid Preparer's Use Only

Preparer's signature | Date | Check if self-employed ▶ ☐ | Preparer's SSN or PTIN
Firm's name (or yours if self-employed), address, and ZIP code ▶ | EIN ▶ | Phone no. ( )

Schedule A Cost of Goods Sold (see page 18 of the instructions)

1 Inventory at beginning of year	1	15,340	
2 Purchases less cost of items withdrawn for personal use	2	256,414	
3 Cost of labor	3		
4 Additional section 263A costs *(attach schedule)*	4		
5 Other costs *(attach schedule)*	5		
6 **Total.** Add lines 1 through 5	6	271,754	
7 Inventory at end of year	7	15,994	
8 **Cost of goods sold.** Subtract line 7 from line 6. Enter here and on page 1, line 2	8	255,760	

9a Check all methods used for valuing closing inventory:

(i) ☐ Cost as described in Regulations section 1.471-3

(ii) ☐ Lower of cost or market as described in Regulations section 1.471-4

(iii) ☐ Other (specify method used and attach explanation) ▶

b Check this box if there was a writedown of "subnormal" goods as described in Regulations section 1.471-2(c). ▶ ☐

c Check this box if the LIFO inventory method was adopted this tax year for any goods *(if checked, attach Form 970)*. ▶ ☐

d Do the rules of section 263A (for property produced or acquired for resale) apply to the partnership? ☐ **Yes** ☐ **No**

e Was there any change in determining quantities, cost, or valuations between opening and closing inventory? ☐ **Yes** ☐ **No**
If "Yes," attach explanation.

Schedule B Other Information

	Yes	No
1 What type of entity is filing this return? Check the applicable box: **a** ☐ Domestic general partnership **b** ☒ Domestic limited partnership **c** ☐ Domestic limited liability company **d** ☐ Domestic limited liability partnership **e** ☐ Foreign partnership **f** ☐ Other ▶		
2 Are any partners in this partnership also partnerships?		X
3 During the partnership's tax year, did the partnership own any interest in another partnership or in any foreign entity that was disregarded as an entity separate from its owner under Regulations sections 301.7701-2 and 301.7701-3? If yes, see instructions for required attachment		X
4 Is this partnership subject to the consolidated audit procedures of sections 6221 through 6233? If "Yes," see **Designation of Tax Matters Partner** below		X
5 Does this partnership meet **all three** of the following requirements? **a** The partnership's total receipts for the tax year were less than $250,000; **b** The partnership's total assets at the end of the tax year were less than $600,000; **and** **c** Schedules K-1 are filed with the return and furnished to the partners on or before the due date (including extensions) for the partnership return. If "Yes," the partnership is not required to complete Schedules L, M-1, and M-2; Item F on page 1 of Form 1065; or Item J on Schedule K-1		X
6 Does this partnership have any foreign partners? If "Yes," the partnership may have to file Forms 8804, 8805 and 8813. See page 20 of the instructions		X
7 Is this partnership a publicly traded partnership as defined in section 469(k)(2)?		X
8 Has this partnership filed, or is it required to file, **Form 8264,** Application for Registration of a Tax Shelter?		X
9 At any time during calendar year 2001, did the partnership have an interest in or a signature or other authority over a financial account in a foreign country (such as a bank account, securities account, or other financial account)? See page 20 of the instructions for exceptions and filing requirements for Form TD F 90-22.1. If "Yes," enter the name of the foreign country. ▶		X
10 During the tax year, did the partnership receive a distribution from, or was it the grantor of, or transferor to, a foreign trust? If "Yes," the partnership may have to file Form 3520. See page 20 of the instructions		X
11 Was there a distribution of property or a transfer (e.g., by sale or death) of a partnership interest during the tax year? If "Yes," you may elect to adjust the basis of the partnership's assets under section 754 by attaching the statement described under **Elections Made By the Partnership** on page 8 of the instructions		X
12 Enter the number of Forms 8865 attached to this return ▶		

Designation of Tax Matters Partner (see page 20 of the instructions)

Enter below the general partner designated as the tax matters partner (TMP) for the tax year of this return:

Name of designated TMP ▶ Ruby Doe

Identifying number of TMP ▶ 123-456-7890

Address of designated TMP ▶ 123 Yellow Brick Road, Any City, OZ 01234

Schedule K Partners' Shares of Income, Credits, Deductions, etc.

Section	(a) Distributive share items	Line	(b) Total amount
Income (Loss)	1 Ordinary income (loss) from trade or business activities (page 1, line 22)	1	60,769
	2 Net income (loss) from rental real estate activities *(attach Form 8825)*	2	
	3a Gross income from other rental activities — 3a		
	b Expenses from other rental activities *(attach schedule)* — 3b		
	c Net income (loss) from other rental activities. Subtract line 3b from line 3a	3c	
	4 Portfolio income (loss): a Interest income	4a	
	b Ordinary dividends	4b	
	c Royalty income	4c	
	d Net short-term capital gain (loss) *(attach Schedule D (Form 1065))*	4d	175
	e (1) Net long-term capital gain (loss) *(attach Schedule D (Form 1065))*	4e(1)	
	(2) 28% rate gain (loss) ▶ (3) Qualified 5-year gain ▶		
	f Other portfolio income (loss) *(attach schedule)*	4f	
	5 Guaranteed payments to partners	5	
	6 Net section 1231 gain (loss) (other than due to casualty or theft) *(attach Form 4797)*	6	
	7 Other income (loss) *(attach schedule)*	7	
Deductions	8 Charitable contributions *(attach schedule)*	8	400
	9 Section 179 expense deduction *(attach Form 4562)*	9	
	10 Deductions related to portfolio income (itemize)	10	
	11 Other deductions *(attach schedule)*	11	
Credits	12a Low-income housing credit:		
	(1) From partnerships to which section 42(j)(5) applies	12a(1)	
	(2) Other than on line 12a(1)	12a(2)	
	b Qualified rehabilitation expenditures related to rental real estate activities *(attach Form 3468)*	12b	
	c Credits (other than credits shown on lines 12a and 12b) related to rental real estate activities	12c	
	d Credits related to other rental activities	12d	
	13 Other credits	13	
Investment Interest	14a Interest expense on investment debts	14a	
	b (1) Investment income included on lines 4a, 4b, 4c, and 4f above	14b(1)	
	(2) Investment expenses included on line 10 above	14b(2)	
Self-Employment	15a Net earnings (loss) from self-employment	15a	
	b Gross farming or fishing income	15b	
	c Gross nonfarm income	15c	
Adjustments and Tax Preference Items	16a Depreciation adjustment on property placed in service after 1986	16a	
	b Adjusted gain or loss	16b	
	c Depletion (other than oil and gas)	16c	
	d (1) Gross income from oil, gas, and geothermal properties	16d(1)	
	(2) Deductions allocable to oil, gas, and geothermal properties	16d(2)	
	e Other adjustments and tax preference items *(attach schedule)*	16e	
Foreign Taxes	17a Name of foreign country or U.S. possession ▶		
	b Gross income from all sources	17b	
	c Gross income sourced at partner level	17c	
	d Foreign gross income sourced at partnership level:		
	(1) Passive ▶ (2) Listed categories *(attach schedule)* ▶ (3) General limitation ▶	17d(3)	
	e Deductions allocated and apportioned at partner level:		
	(1) Interest expense ▶ (2) Other ▶	17e(2)	
	f Deductions allocated and apportioned at partnership level to foreign source income:		
	(1) Passive ▶ (2) Listed categories *(attach schedule)* ▶ (3) General limitation ▶	17f(3)	
	g Total foreign taxes (check one): ▶ Paid ☐ Accrued ☐	17g	
	h Reduction in taxes available for credit *(attach schedule)*	17h	
Other	18 Section 59(e)(2) expenditures: a Type ▶ b Amount ▶	18b	
	19 Tax-exempt interest income	19	45
	20 Other tax-exempt income	20	
	21 Nondeductible expenses	21	
	22 Distributions of money (cash and marketable securities)	22	51,300
	23 Distributions of property other than money	23	
	24 Other items and amounts required to be reported separately to partners *(attach schedule)*		

Analysis of Net Income (Loss)

1	Net income (loss). Combine Schedule K, lines 1 through 7 in column (b). From the result, subtract the sum of Schedule K, lines 8 through 11, 14a, 17g, and 18b	1	60,544

2 Analysis by partner type:	(i) Corporate	(ii) Individual (active)	(iii) Individual (passive)	(iv) Partnership	(v) Exempt organization	(vi) Nominee/Other
a General partners						
b Limited partners						

Schedule L — Balance Sheets per Books (Not required if Question 5 on Schedule B is answered "Yes.")

Assets	Beginning of tax year (a)	(b)	End of tax year (c)	(d)
1 Cash		9,683		
2a Trade notes and accounts receivable	7,025		9,905	
b Less allowance for bad debts		15,340		15,994
3 Inventories				
4 U.S. government obligations		900		900
5 Tax-exempt securities				
6 Other current assets *(attach schedule)*				
7 Mortgage and real estate loans				
8 Other investments *(attach schedule)*		1,000		1,000
9a Buildings and other depreciable assets	4,802		4,802	
b Less accumulated depreciation				
10a Depletable assets				
b Less accumulated depletion				
11 Land (net of any amortization)				
12a Intangible assets (amortizable only)				
b Less accumulated amortization				
13 Other assets *(attach schedule)*				
14 **Total** assets		38,750		41,684
Liabilities and Capital				
15 Accounts payable		10,212		10,111
16 Mortgages, notes, bonds payable in less than 1 year		3,600		3000
17 Other current liabilities *(attach schedule)*				
18 All nonrecourse loans				
19 Mortgages, notes, bonds payable in 1 year or more				7,593
20 Other liabilities *(attach schedule)*				
21 Partners' capital accounts		24,938		20,980
22 **Total** liabilities and capital				41,684

Schedule M-1 — Reconciliation of Income (Loss) per Books With Income (Loss) per Return (Not required if Question 5 on Schedule B is answered "Yes.")

1 Net income (loss) per books	35,589	6 Income recorded on books this year not included on Schedule K, lines 1 through 7 (itemize): a Tax-exempt interest $	45
2 Income included on Schedule K, lines 1 through 4, 6, and 7, not recorded on books this year (itemize):		7 Deductions included on Schedule K, lines 1 through 11, 14a, 17g, and 18b, not charged against book income this year (itemize): a Depreciation $	
3 Guaranteed payments (other than health insurance)	25,000		
4 Expenses recorded on books this year not included on Schedule K, lines 1 through 11, 14a, 17g, and 18b (itemize): a Depreciation $ b Travel and entertainment $		8 Add lines 6 and 7	45
5 Add lines 1 through 4	60,589	9 Income (loss) (Analysis of Net Income (Loss), line 1). Subtract line 8 from line 5	60,544

Schedule M-2 — Analysis of Partners' Capital Accounts (Not required if Question 5 on Schedule B is answered "Yes.")

1 Balance at beginning of year	24,938	6 Distributions: a Cash	51,350
2 Capital contributed during year		b Property	
3 Net income (loss) per books	35,589	7 Other decreases (itemize):	
4 Other increases (itemize):		8 Add lines 6 and 7	51,350
5 Add lines 1 through 4	60,527	9 Balance at end of year. Subtract line 8 from line 5	9,177

form 13

SCHEDULE K-1 (Form 1065)
Department of the Treasury
Internal Revenue Service

Partner's Share of Income, Credits, Deductions, etc.

▶ See separate instructions.

For calendar year 2001 or tax year beginning , 2001, and ending , 20

OMB No. 1545-0099

2001

Partner's identifying number ▶ 123-45-6789

Partnership's identifying number ▶ 60,544

Partner's name, address, and ZIP code

Ruby Doe
123 Yellow Brick Road
Any City, OZ 01234

Partnership's name, address, and ZIP code

Ruby's Slippers, Ltd.
123 Yellow Brick Rd
Any City, OZ 01234

A This partner is a ☒ general partner ☐ limited partner ☐ limited liability company member

B What type of entity is this partner? ▶ individual

C Is this partner a ☒ domestic or a ☐ foreign partner?

D Enter partner's percentage of:

	(i) Before change or termination	(ii) End of year
Profit sharing	33 %	33 %
Loss sharing	33 %	33 %
Ownership of capital	33 %	33 %

E IRS Center where partnership filed return:

F Partner's share of liabilities (see instructions):
Nonrecourse . . . $
Qualified nonrecourse financing . . $
Other . . . $

G Tax shelter registration number . . ▶

H Check here if this partnership is a publicly traded partnership as defined in section 469(k)(2) . . . ☐

I Check applicable boxes: (1) ☒ Final K-1 (2) ☐ Amended K-1

J Analysis of partner's capital account:

(a) Capital account at beginning of year	(b) Capital contributed during year	(c) Partner's share of lines 3, 4, and 7, Form 1065, Schedule M-2	(d) Withdrawals and distributions	(e) Capital account at end of year (combine columns (a) through (d))
			( )	

		(a) Distributive share item		(b) Amount	(c) 1040 filers enter the amount in column (b) on:
Income (Loss)	1	Ordinary income (loss) from trade or business activities	1	60,769	See page 6 of Partner's Instructions for Schedule K-1 (Form 1065).
	2	Net income (loss) from rental real estate activities	2		
	3	Net income (loss) from other rental activities	3		
	4	Portfolio income (loss):			
	a	Interest	4a		Sch. B, Part I, line 1
	b	Ordinary dividends	4b		Sch. B, Part II, line 5
	c	Royalties	4c		Sch. E, Part I, line 4
	d	Net short-term capital gain (loss)	4d		Sch. D, line 5, col. (f)
	e	(1) Net long-term capital gain (loss)	4e(1)		Sch. D, line 12, col. (f)
		(2) 28% rate gain (loss)	4e(2)		Sch. D, line 12, col. (g)
		(3) Qualified 5-year gain	4e(3)		Line 4 of worksheet for Sch. D, line 29
	f	Other portfolio income (loss) *(attach schedule)*	4f		Enter on applicable line of your return.
	5	Guaranteed payments to partner	5	25,000	See page 6 of Partner's Instructions for Schedule K-1 (Form 1065).
	6	Net section 1231 gain (loss) (other than due to casualty or theft)	6		
	7	Other income (loss) *(attach schedule)*	7		Enter on applicable line of your return.
Deductions	8	Charitable contributions (see instructions) *(attach schedule)*	8	400	Sch. A, line 15 or 16
	9	Section 179 expense deduction	9		See pages 7 and 8 of Partner's Instructions for Schedule K-1 (Form 1065).
	10	Deductions related to portfolio income *(attach schedule)*	10		
	11	Other deductions *(attach schedule)*	11		
Credits	12a	Low-income housing credit:			
		(1) From section 42(j)(5) partnerships	12a(1)		Form 8586, line 5
		(2) Other than on line 12a(1)	12a(2)		
	b	Qualified rehabilitation expenditures related to rental real estate activities	12b		See page 8 of Partner's Instructions for Schedule K-1 (Form 1065).
	c	Credits (other than credits shown on lines 12a and 12b) related to rental real estate activities	12c		
	d	Credits related to other rental activities	12d		
	13	Other credits	13		

For Paperwork Reduction Act Notice, see Instructions for Form 1065. Cat. No. 11394R **Schedule K-1 (Form 1065) 2001**

	(a) Distributive share item		(b) Amount	(c) 1040 filers enter the amount in column (b) on:
Investment Interest	14a Interest expense on investment debts	14a		Form 4952, line 1
	b (1) Investment income included on lines 4a, 4b, 4c, and 4f	14b(1)	175	See page 9 of Partner's Instructions for Schedule K-1 (Form 1065).
	(2) Investment expenses included on line 10	14b(2)		
Self-employment	15a Net earnings (loss) from self-employment	15a		Sch. SE, Section A or B
	b Gross farming or fishing income	15b		See page 9 of Partner's Instructions for Schedule K-1 (Form 1065).
	c Gross nonfarm income	15c		
Adjustments and Tax Preference Items	16a Depreciation adjustment on property placed in service after 1986	16a		See page 9 of Partner's Instructions for Schedule K-1 (Form 1065) and Instructions for Form 6251.
	b Adjusted gain or loss	16b		
	c Depletion (other than oil and gas)	16c		
	d (1) Gross income from oil, gas, and geothermal properties	16d(1)		
	(2) Deductions allocable to oil, gas, and geothermal properties	16d(2)		
	e Other adjustments and tax preference items *(attach schedule)*	16e		
Foreign Taxes	17a Name of foreign country or U.S. possession ▶			Form 1116, Part I
	b Gross income from all sources	17b		
	c Gross income sourced at partner level	17c		
	d Foreign gross income sourced at partnership level:			
	(1) Passive	17d(1)		
	(2) Listed categories *(attach schedule)*	17d(2)		
	(3) General limitation	17d(3)		
	e Deductions allocated and apportioned at partner level:			
	(1) Interest expense	17e(1)		
	(2) Other	17e(2)		
	f Deductions allocated and apportioned at partnership level to foreign source income:			
	(1) Passive	17f(1)		
	(2) Listed categories *(attach schedule)*	17f(2)		
	(3) General limitation	17f(3)		
	g Total foreign taxes (check one): ▶ ☐ Paid ☐ Accrued	17g		Form 1116, Part II
	h Reduction in taxes available for credit *(attach schedule)*	17h		Form 1116, line 12
Other	18 Section 59(e)(2) expenditures: **a** Type ▶			See page 9 of Partner's Instructions for Schedule K-1 (Form 1065).
	b Amount	18b		
	19 Tax-exempt interest income	19	45	Form 1040, line 8b
	20 Other tax-exempt income	20		See pages 9 and 10 of Partner's Instructions for Schedule K-1 (Form 1065).
	21 Nondeductible expenses	21		
	22 Distributions of money (cash and marketable securities)	22	51,350	
	23 Distributions of property other than money	23		
	24 Recapture of low-income housing credit:			
	a From section 42(j)(5) partnerships	24a		Form 8611, line 8
	b Other than on line 24a	24b		

Supplemental Information

25 Supplemental information required to be reported separately to each partner *(attach additional schedules if more space is needed):*

Form 1040 — U.S. Individual Income Tax Return 2001

Department of the Treasury—Internal Revenue Service (99) IRS Use Only—Do not write or staple in this space.

For the year Jan. 1–Dec. 31, 2001, or other tax year beginning , 2001, ending , 20 — OMB No. 1545-0074

Label (See instructions on page 19.) **Use the IRS label.** Otherwise, please print or type.

LABEL HERE

Your first name and initial: Anita	Last name: Refund	Your social security number: 000 11 2345
If a joint return, spouse's first name and initial	Last name	Spouse's social security number
Home address (number and street). If you have a P.O. box, see page 19.: 1040 Deduction St.	Apt. no.	**Important!** You **must** enter your SSN(s) above.
City, town or post office, state, and ZIP code. If you have a foreign address, see page 19.: Greenback, Il 60000		

Presidential Election Campaign (See page 19.)
Note. Checking "Yes" will not change your tax or reduce your refund.
Do you, or your spouse if filing a joint return, want $3 to go to this fund? ▶ You ☐ Yes ☒ No Spouse ☐ Yes ☐ No

Filing Status

Check only one box.

1. ☐ Single
2. ☐ Married filing joint return (even if only one had income)
3. ☐ Married filing separate return. Enter spouse's social security no. above and full name here. ▶
4. ☐ Head of household (with qualifying person). (See page 19.) If the qualifying person is a child but not your dependent, enter this child's name here. ▶
5. ☐ Qualifying widow(er) with dependent child (year spouse died ▶). (See page 19.)

Exemptions

6a ☒ **Yourself.** If your parent (or someone else) can claim you as a dependent on his or her tax return, **do not** check box 6a — No. of boxes checked on 6a and 6b: 1

b ☐ **Spouse**

c **Dependents:**

If more than six dependents, see page 20.

(1) First name Last name	(2) Dependent's social security number	(3) Dependent's relationship to you	(4)✓ if qualifying child for child tax credit (see page 20)
			☐
			☐
			☐
			☐
			☐
			☐

No. of your children on 6c who:
- lived with you: 0
- did not live with you due to divorce or separation (see page 20): 0

Dependents on 6c not entered above: 0

d Total number of exemptions claimed — Add numbers entered on lines above ▶ 1

Income

Attach Forms W-2 and W-2G here. Also attach Form(s) 1099-R if tax was withheld.

If you did not get a W-2, see page 21.

Enclose, but do not attach, any payment. Also, please use Form 1040-V.

7	Wages, salaries, tips, etc. Attach Form(s) W-2	7	72,251
8a	**Taxable** interest. Attach Schedule B if required	8a	456
b	**Tax-exempt** interest. **Do not** include on line 8a — 8b		
9	Ordinary dividends. Attach Schedule B if required	9	1,028
10	Taxable refunds, credits, or offsets of state and local income taxes (see page 22)	10	775
11	Alimony received	11	
12	Business income or (loss). Attach Schedule C or C-EZ	12	
13	Capital gain or (loss). Attach Schedule D if required. If not required, check here ▶ ☐	13	
14	Other gains or (losses). Attach Form 4797	14	
15a	Total IRA distributions — 15a — b Taxable amount (see page 23)	15b	
16a	Total pensions and annuities — 16a — b Taxable amount (see page 23)	16b	
17	Rental real estate, royalties, partnerships, S corporations, trusts, etc. Attach Schedule E	17	
18	Farm income or (loss). Attach Schedule F	18	
19	Unemployment compensation	19	
20a	Social security benefits — 20a — b Taxable amount (see page 25)	20b	
21	Other income. List type and amount (see page 27)	21	
22	Add the amounts in the far right column for lines 7 through 21. This is your **total income** ▶	22	74,510

Adjusted Gross Income

Line	Description		Amount		Amount
23	IRA deduction (see page 27)	23	225		
24	Student loan interest deduction (see page 28)	24			
25	Archer MSA deduction. Attach Form 8853	25			
26	Moving expenses. Attach Form 3903	26			
27	One-half of self-employment tax. Attach Schedule SE	27			
28	Self-employed health insurance deduction (see page 30)	28			
29	Self-employed SEP, SIMPLE, and qualified plans	29			
30	Penalty on early withdrawal of savings	30			
31a	Alimony paid b Recipient's SSN ▶	31a			
32	Add lines 23 through 31a			32	225
33	Subtract line 32 from line 22. This is your **adjusted gross income** ▶			33	74,285

Tax and Credits

Standard Deduction for-
- People who checked any box on line 35a or 35b **or** who can be claimed as a dependent, see page 31.
- All others:

Single, $4,550

Head of household, $6,650

Married filing jointly or Qualifying widow(er), $7,600

Married filing separately, $3,800

Line	Description		Amount
34	Amount from line 33 (adjusted gross income)		34: 74,285
35a	Check if: ☐ **You** were 65 or older, ☐ Blind; ☐ **Spouse** was 65 or older, ☐ Blind. Add the number of boxes checked above and enter the total here ▶ 35a		
b	If you are married filing separately and your spouse itemizes deductions, or you were a dual-status alien, see page 31 and check here ▶ 35b ☐		
36	**Itemized deductions** (from Schedule A) **or** your **standard deduction** (see left margin)		36: 4550
37	Subtract line 36 from line 34		37: 69,785
38	If line 34 is $99,725 or less, multiply $2,900 by the total number of exemptions claimed on line 6d. If line 34 is over $99,725, see the worksheet on page 32		38: 2900
39	**Taxable income.** Subtract line 38 from line 37. If line 38 is more than line 37, enter -0-		39: 66,835
40	**Tax** (see page 33). Check if any tax is from **a** ☐ Form(s) 8814 **b** ☐ Form 4972		40: 14,389
41	**Alternative minimum tax** (see page 34). Attach Form 6251		41: 0
42	Add lines 40 and 41 ▶		42: 14,389
43	Foreign tax credit. Attach Form 1116 if required	43:	
44	Credit for child and dependent care expenses. Attach Form 2441	44:	
45	Credit for the elderly or the disabled. Attach Schedule R	45:	
46	Education credits. Attach Form 8863	46: 1,000	
47	Rate reduction credit. See the worksheet on page 36	47:	
48	Child tax credit (see page 37)	48:	
49	Adoption credit. Attach Form 8839	49:	
50	Other credits from: **a** ☐ Form 3800 **b** ☐ Form 8396 **c** ☐ Form 8801 **d** ☐ Form (specify) ____	50:	
51	Add lines 43 through 50. These are your **total credits**		51: 1,000
52	Subtract line 51 from line 42. If line 51 is more than line 42, enter -0- ▶		52: 13,389

Other Taxes

Line	Description		Amount
53	Self-employment tax. Attach Schedule SE		53:
54	Social security and Medicare tax on tip income not reported to employer. Attach Form 4137		54:
55	Tax on qualified plans, including IRAs, and other tax-favored accounts. Attach Form 5329 if required		55:
56	Advance earned income credit payments from Form(s) W-2		56:
57	Household employment taxes. Attach Schedule H		57:
58	Add lines 52 through 57. This is your **total tax** ▶		58: 13,389

Payments

If you have a qualifying child, attach Schedule EIC.

59	Federal income tax withheld from Forms W-2 and 1099	59: 14,450	
60	2001 estimated tax payments and amount applied from 2000 return	60:	
61a	**Earned income credit (EIC)**	61a:	
b	Nontaxable earned income 61b		
62	Excess social security and RRTA tax withheld (see page 51)	62:	
63	Additional child tax credit. Attach Form 8812	63:	
64	Amount paid with request for extension to file (see page 51)	64:	
65	Other payments. Check if from **a** ☐ Form 2439 **b** ☐ Form 4136	65:	
66	Add lines 59, 60, 61a, and 62 through 65. These are your **total payments** ▶		66: 14,450

Refund

Direct deposit? See page 51 and fill in 68b, 68c, and 68d.

67	If line 66 is more than line 58, subtract line 58 from line 66. This is the amount you **overpaid**		67: 1,061
68a	Amount of line 67 you want **refunded to you** ▶		68a: 1,061
b	Routing number 001122333 ▶ **c** Type: ☒ Checking ☐ Savings		
d	Account number 12345678909876543		
69	Amount of line 67 you want **applied to your 2002 estimated tax** ▶	69: 0	

Amount You Owe

Line	Description		Amount
70	**Amount you owe.** Subtract line 66 from line 58. For details on how to pay, see page 52 ▶		70: 0
71	Estimated tax penalty. Also include on line 70	71:	

Third Party Designee

Do you want to allow another person to discuss this return with the IRS (see page 53)? ☐ **Yes.** Complete the following. ☐ **No**

Designee's name ▶ Phone no. ▶ ( ) Personal identification number (PIN) ▶

Sign Here

Joint return? See page 19. Keep a copy for your records.

Under penalties of perjury, I declare that I have examined this return and accompanying schedules and statements, and to the best of my knowledge and belief, they are true, correct, and complete. Declaration of preparer (other than taxpayer) is based on all information of which preparer has any knowledge.

Your signature	Date	Your occupation	Daytime phone number
Anita Refund	4-12-04	teacher	(555) 555-6789
Spouse's signature. If a joint return, **both** must sign.	Date	Spouse's occupation	

Paid Preparer's Use Only

Preparer's signature	Date	Check if self-employed ☐	Preparer's SSN or PTIN
Firm's name (or yours if self-employed), address, and ZIP code		EIN	
		Phone no. ( )	

form 15

SCHEDULE E (Form 1040)

Department of the Treasury
Internal Revenue Service (99)

Supplemental Income and Loss

(From rental real estate, royalties, partnerships, S corporations, estates, trusts, REMICs, etc.)

▶ Attach to Form 1040 or Form 1041. ▶ See Instructions for Schedule E (Form 1040).

OMB No. 1545-0074

2001

Attachment Sequence No. 13

Name(s) shown on return: Frank N. Stein

Your social security number: 123 45 6789

Part I Income or Loss From Rental Real Estate and Royalties **Note.** If you are in the business of renting personal property, use **Schedule C** or **C-EZ** (see page E-1). Report farm rental income or loss from **Form 4835** on page 2, line 39.

1	Show the kind and location of each **rental real estate property:**
A	
B	
C	

2 For each rental real estate property listed on line 1, did you or your family use it during the tax year for personal purposes for more than the greater of:
- 14 days **or**
- 10% of the total days rented at fair rental value?

(See page E-1.)

	Yes	No
A		
B		
C		

Income:		Properties A	Properties B	Properties C	Totals (Add columns A, B, and C.)
3 Rents received	3				3
4 Royalties received	4				4
Expenses:					
5 Advertising	5				
6 Auto and travel (see page E-2)	6				
7 Cleaning and maintenance	7				
8 Commissions	8				
9 Insurance	9				
10 Legal and other professional fees	10				
11 Management fees	11				
12 Mortgage interest paid to banks, etc. (see page E-2)	12				12
13 Other interest	13				
14 Repairs	14				
15 Supplies	15				
16 Taxes	16				
17 Utilities	17				
18 Other (list) ▶	18				
19 Add lines 5 through 18	19				19
20 Depreciation expense or depletion (see page E-3)	20				20
21 Total expenses. Add lines 19 and 20	21				
22 Income or (loss) from rental real estate or royalty properties. Subtract line 21 from line 3 (rents) or line 4 (royalties). If the result is a (loss), see page E-3 to find out if you must file **Form 6198**	22				
23 Deductible rental real estate loss. **Caution.** Your rental real estate loss on line 22 may be limited. See page E-3 to find out if you must file **Form 8582.** Real estate professionals must complete line 42 on page 2	23	( )	( )	( )	

24	**Income.** Add positive amounts shown on line 22. **Do not** include any losses	24
25	**Losses.** Add royalty losses from line 22 and rental real estate losses from line 23. Enter total losses here	25 ( )
26	**Total rental real estate and royalty income or (loss).** Combine lines 24 and 25. Enter the result here. If Parts II, III, IV, and line 39 on page 2 do not apply to you, also enter this amount on Form 1040, line 17. Otherwise, include this amount in the total on line 40 on page 2	26

Name(s) shown on return. Do not enter name and social security number if shown on other side.
Frank N. Stein

Your social security number
123 45 6789

Note. If you report amounts from farming or fishing on Schedule E, you must enter your gross income from those activities on line 41 below. Real estate professionals must complete line 42 below.

Part II Income or Loss From Partnerships and S Corporations

Note. If you report a loss from an at-risk activity, you **must** check either column **(e)** or **(f)** on line 27 to describe your investment in the activity. See page E-5. If you check column **(f)**, you must attach **Form 6198.**

27	(a) Name	(b) Enter P for partnership; S for S corporation	(c) Check if foreign partnership	(d) Employer identification number	Investment At Risk? (e) All is at risk	(f) Some is not at risk
A	Frank's Costumes Ltd.	P		01-234567878	x	
B						
C						
D						
E						

	Passive Income and Loss		Nonpassive Income and Loss		
	(g) Passive loss allowed (attach Form 8582 if required)	(h) Passive income from Schedule K-1	(i) Nonpassive loss from Schedule K-1	(j) Section 179 expense deduction from Form 4562	(k) Nonpassive income from Schedule K-1
A	1964	2386	864	386	25,986
B					
C					
D					
E					
28a Totals		2836			
b Totals	1964		864	386	

29	Add columns (h) and (k) of line 28a	29	25,986
30	Add columns (g), (i), and (j) of line 28b	30	(3214)
31	Total partnership and S corporation income or (loss). Combine lines 29 and 30. Enter the result here and include in the total on line 40 below	31	25,158

Part III Income or Loss From Estates and Trusts

32	(a) Name	(b) Employer identification number
A		
B		

	Passive Income and Loss		Nonpassive Income and Loss	
	(c) Passive deduction or loss allowed (attach Form 8582 if required)	(d) Passive income from Schedule K-1	(e) Deduction or loss from Schedule K-1	(f) Other income from Schedule K-1
A				
B				
33a Totals				
b Totals				

34	Add columns (d) and (f) of line 33a	34	
35	Add columns (c) and (e) of line 33b	35	( )
36	Total estate and trust income or (loss). Combine lines 34 and 35. Enter the result here and include in the total on line 40 below	36	

Part IV Income or Loss From Real Estate Mortgage Investment Conduits (REMICs)- Residual Holder

37	(a) Name	(b) Employer identification number	(c) Excess inclusion from Schedules Q, line 2c (see page E-6)	(d) Taxable income (net loss) from Schedules Q, line 1b	(e) Income from Schedules Q, line 3b

38	Combine columns (d) and (e) only. Enter the result here and include in the total on line 40 below	38	

Part V Summary

39	Net farm rental income or (loss) from **Form 4835**. Also, complete line 41 below	39	
40	**Total** income or (loss). Combine lines 26, 31, 36, 38, and 39. Enter the result here and on Form 1040, line 17 ▶	40	25,158
41	**Reconciliation of Farming and Fishing Income.** Enter your **gross** farming and fishing income reported on Form 4835, line 7; Schedule K-1 (Form 1065), line 15b; Schedule K-1 (Form 1120S), line 23; and Schedule K-1 (Form 1041), line 14 (see page E-6)	41	
42	**Reconciliation for Real Estate Professionals.** If you were a real estate professional (see page E-4), enter the net income or (loss) you reported anywhere on Form 1040 from all rental real estate activities in which you materially participated under the passive activity loss rules	42	

Appendix F
Blank Forms

You may use these blank forms in starting, running, and changing the structure of your FLP.

Table of Forms

TRANSMITTAL LETTER

Secretary of State
(ADDRESS)

SUBJECT: ______________________________
(Proposed family limited partnership name)

Enclosed are two (2) originals and one (1) copy of the Certificate of Limited Partnership and a check in the amount of $_____________ which represents the filing fee for a limited partnership.

Please return the enclosed photocopy to me with the filing date stamped on it.

FROM: __________________________
Name (printed or typed)

____
Street Address

____
City, State & Zip Code

____
Daytime telephone number

This page intentionally left blank.

Certificate of Assumed Name

The undersigned hereby certify the following:

1. The undersigned are conducting business as partners of a limited partnership under the laws of the State of ________________. The business conducted by the limited partnership is ____ under the name of ____ and it principal place of business is located at ____.

2. The real names and residences of all of the partners of the limited partnership are:

   General Partner: ____

   Limited Partners: ____

   ____

   ____

3. No other person is interested as a partner, part owner, or otherwise in the business or conduct of it.

This Certificate is executed and filed pursuant to state law relating to the conduct of business under a Fictitious/Assumed name.

SIGNED this _________ day of ___________________________, 20______.

____

Partner

____

Partner

____

Partner

STATE OF ____________________ §
§
COUNTY OF _________________ §

On this ______ day of ________________, 20_______, before me personally appeared ___________________________, known to me to be the person whose name is subscribed to this Certificate and acknowledged to me that he/she executed the same in his/her authorized capacity as general partner of ______________________________, and that by his/her signature on this Certificate the person or entity upon whose behalf the he/she acted, executed the Certificate.

____
Notary Public
State of ____________________________
My commission expires:_______________

STATE OF ____________________ §
§
COUNTY OF _________________ §

On this ______ day of ________________, 20_______, before me personally appeared ___________________________, known to me to be the person whose name is subscribed to this Certificate and acknowledged to me that he/she executed the same in his/her authorized capacity as limited partner of ______________________________________, and that by his/her signature on this Certificate the person or entity upon whose behalf the he/she acted, executed the Certificate.

____
Notary Public
State of ____________________________
My commission expires:_______________

STATE OF ____________________ §
§
COUNTY OF _________________ §

On this ______ day of ________________, 20_______, before me personally appeared ___________________________, known to me to be the person whose name is subscribed to this Certificate and acknowledged to me that he/she executed the same in his/her authorized capacity as limited partner of ______________________________, and that by his/her signature on this Certificate the person or entity upon whose behalf the he/she acted, executed the Certificate.

____
Notary Public
State of ____________________________
My commission expires:_______________

CERTIFICATE OF LIMITED PARTNERSHIP

The partners of ________________________________, a limited partnership formed under the laws of the State of _______________, (hereinafter "Partnership"), hereby execute the following Certificate of Limited Partnership.

1. **Name of the Partnership**. The name of the Partnership is: ________________________________.

2. **Registered Agent**. The registered agent for service of process for the Partnership is: ________________________________.

3. **Registered Office**. The registered office of the Partnership is located at the following address: ____________________________.

4. **Name and address of General Partner**. The name(s) and address(es) of each general partner of the Partnership at the time of the original admission to the Partnership of such partner are the following:

GENERAL PARTNER	BUSINESS RESIDENCE OR MAILING ADDRESS

5. **Partners**. There are at least two partners in the Partnership at least one of whom is a limited partner.

6. **Duration**. The Partnership shall continue for _______ (____) years.

7. **Effective Date**. The Partnership shall be deemed formed on the date that this Certificate of Limited Partnership is filed in the office of the Secretary of State.

SIGNED this _______ day of _____________, 20______.

GENERAL PARTNER(S):

________________________________ ________________________________

________________________________ ________________________________

This page intentionally left blank.

PARTNERSHIP AGREEMENT
OF

____
a Limited Partnership

The Partnership Agreement is made this ______ day of ____________, 20_____, by and between ______________________, ______________________, and ____________________ (individually the "Partner" and collectively the "Partners").

In consideration of the mutual terms, conditions and covenants hereinafter set forth, the Partners agree as follows:

I. GENERAL

1.1 The purpose of the Partnership shall be ______________________________________.

1.2 The name of the Partnership shall be ______________________, (the "Partnership").

1.3 The Partnership shall be operated as a limited partnership under the laws of the State of ____________________________.

1.4 The initial address of the Partnership shall be ____________________________, which may be changed from time to time by the Partners.

1.5 The Partners shall execute the necessary documents to register the Partnership name and existence with the proper governmental offices in the County of __________________, State of ________________________.

1.6 The Partnership shall continue until, and dissolve upon, the first happening of:

a. The death of one Partner; or

b. The withdrawal, by written notice, of one Partner; or

c. The affirmative vote of a majority in interest of the Limited Partners.

II. CAPITALIZATION

2.1 The Partners shall contribute to the Partnership in the following amounts which shall reflect their Partnership interest:

____________________	$____________________	____________________%
____________________	$____________________	____________________%
____________________	$____________________	____________________%
____________________	$____________________	____________________%

2.2 No Partner shall receive interest on his capital contribution.

2.3 A separate "Capital Account" shall be maintained for each Partner.

a. A Capital Account shall be increased by (1) the contribution to the capital of the Partnership, including the initial contribution (Paragraph 2.1 above) and (2) the distributive share of the Net Profits of the Partnership; and decreased by (1) distributions, (2) the distributive share of Net Losses of the Partnership and (3) the distributive share of expenditures of the Partnership not deductible in computing Net Profits/Losses and not properly treated as capital expenditures.

b. Distributions in kind shall be valued at fair market value less any liability which the Partner assumes on the distribution or to which the asset distributed is subject.

2.4 If in the opinion of the majority in interest of the Limited Partners of the Partnership additional capital is needed for the proper conduct of the business of the Partnership, each Partner shall contribute pro rata in accordance with his interest.

2.5 No Limited Partner shall be liable for any obligation incurred by the General Partner on behalf of the Partnership. No Limited Partner shall be responsible for payment of any amount due a creditor of the Partnership.

III. MANAGEMENT

3.1 All matters to be determined by the Partners shall be determined by the affirmative vote of a majority in interest of the Limited Partners present at a meeting of the Partnership. All matters determined by the Partners shall be recorded in a Minute Book reflecting the date, matter discussed and the action taken.

3.2 The Partners shall meet at least once each year. Additional meetings may be held at the request of 66 2/3% of the Partnership by interest. All meetings shall be by written notice reasonably in advance of such meeting so that each Partner may be present either in person or by written proxy authorization.

3.3 At the first meeting of the Partnership to be held on ______________________, at ______________________, at ________ p.m./a.m., the Partnership shall determine:

a. the manner in which the business of the Partnership shall be managed;

b. the hiring of employees;

c. salaries to be paid to employees and the General Partner who participates in the day-to-day management of the business of the Partnership;

d. banking procedures; and

e. any other matters which may properly come before the Partnership.

3.4 The fiscal year of the Partnership shall end December 31.

3.5 Each Partner shall have the right to inspect the books, records, reports and accounts of the Partnership during normal business hours, which books, records, reports and accounts shall be kept at the Partnership's place of business or at such other place as determined from time to time by the Partnership.

IV. RESTRICTIONS

4.1 No Partner shall sell, assign, mortgage, hypothecate or encumber his interest in the Partnership without the express written permission of all the remaining Partners, without regard to interest.

4.2 All Partners shall meet their personal obligations and debts as they become due and each agrees to save and hold remaining Partners and the Partnership harmless from all costs, claims and demands with respect to such obligations and debts.

4.3 No Limited Partner shall:

a. lend any Partnership funds;

b incur any obligation in the name of or on the credit of the Partnership;

c. lend any of the Partner's funds to the Partnership, with or without interest;

d. sell, assign, mortgage, hypothecate or encumber any asset of the Partnership;

e. make an assignment of the assets of the Partnership for the benefit of creditors of the Partnership;

f. execute any guarantee on behalf of the Partnership;

g. release, assign or transfer a Partnership claim or any asset of the Partnership;

h. borrow in the name of the Partnership;

i. Submit any Partnership claim or liability in arbitration;

j. initiate, conduct or settle litigation in the name of or pertaining to the Partnership; or

k. invest Partnership funds or other assets.

4.4 Any Partner who commits a prohibited act shall be individually liable to the remaining Partners, pro rata to their Partnership interest, for any loss caused by the prohibited act.

V. PROFITS/LOSSES AND DISTRIBUTIONS

5.1 Net Profits/Losses shall be determined in accordance with good accounting principles and shall be as finally determined for federal income tax purposes.

5.2 Net Profits/Losses shall be apportioned pro rata among the Partners' capital account according to each Partner's interest.

5.3 Distribution shall be made upon the recommendation of the General Partner.

VI. ADDITIONAL PARTNERS/DISSOLUTION

6.1 The Partnership may admit additional Partners upon the affirmative vote of the Limited Partners, as provided herein. Additional Partners shall then be admitted upon payment of a contribution to capital as determined by the Partnership and each Partner's interest in the Partnership as provided for in paragraph 2.1 shall be redetermined.

6.2 In the event of the dissolution of the Partnership for any reason, the affairs of the Partnership shall be wound up and the proceeds of the Partnership distributed in accordance with the terms of this Agreement and the laws of the State of ____________________.

VII. MISCELLANEOUS

7.1 If any controversy or claim arising out of this Agreement cannot be settled by the Partners, the controversy or claims shall be settled by arbitration in the City of _______________, State of _______________, in accordance with the rules of the American Arbitration Association then in effect, and judgment on the award my be entered in any court having jurisdiction.

7.2 This Agreement shall be enforced and construed under and shall be subject to the laws of the State of _______________. If any provision of this Agreement shall be unlawful, void or unenforceable, that provision shall be deemed separate from and in no way shall affect the validity or enforceability of the remaining provisions of this Agreement.

7.3 All notices required to be given under this Agreement shall be either (1) personally delivered to the party to whom addressed or (2) sent by U.S. Mail, postage prepaid, Certified mail, Return Receipt Requested, addressed to the Partner at the last address for that Partner as maintained by the Partnership.

7.4 This Agreement contains the full and complete understanding of all of the Partners with reference to the Partnership and supercedes all prior agreements and understandings, whether written or oral. This Areement may not be amended except in writing and upon the consent of all of the Partners then existing of the Partnership.

7.5 This Agreement shall be binding on and inure to the benefit of the respective successors, permitted assigns, executors, administrators, personal representatives and beneficiaries of the Partners.

EXECUTED by the Partners as of the date first above written.

____
General Partner

____
Limited Partner

____
Limited Partner

This page intentionally left blank.

Sale of Partnership Interest to Partners

Date: ______________________

TO: ______________________

____

____

Partners:

In consideration of the sum of $____________ to be paid by me upon the execution of this Agreement of Sale of a Partnership Interest, we agree as follows:

1. I hereby sell and transfer my entire interest as a partner in ____________________, a limited partnership organized under the laws of the State of __________ ("Partnership") to be divided among you as you may determine.

2. Have no objection to, and grant you the right to continue to do business under the partnership name of ____________________________________.

3. It is understood that I shall have the right to engage in a business similar to that engaged in by the Partnership and that nothing contained herein shall be deemed a covenant on my part not to compete.

4. There shall be a public announcement communicated to all those with whom the Partnership has done business in the past that I am no longer a member of the Partnership.

5. Each of us hereby releases the other from all past and present claims or obligations whatsoever as between the Partnership, each of you, and myself.

IN WITNESS WHEREOF the parties have signed this Agreement.

____
General Partner

____
Limited Partner

____
Limited Partner

This page intentionally left blank.

General Assignment

BE IT KNOWN, for value received, the undersigned ____________________, of ____________________ hereby unconditionally and irrevocably assigns and transfers unto ____________________, a limited partnership formed and operated under the laws of the State of ________________________, all right, title and interest to the following property:

The undersigned fully warrants that it has full rights and authority to enter into this assignment and that the rights and benefits hereunder assigned are free and clear of any lien, encumbrance, adverse claim or interest by any third party.

This assignment shall be binding upon and inure to the benefit of the parties, and their successors and assigns.

SIGNED this __________ day of __________________________, 20_____.

______________________________ Witness

______________________________ Assignor

GENERAL PARTNER OF
LIMITED PARTNERSHIP:

______________________________ Witness

____

This page intentionally left blank.

QUITCLAIM DEED

THIS QUITCLAIM DEED, executed this _____ day of _________, 20_____, by ____________________, the Grantor, whose post office address is:____ to ____________________________, the Grantee, a limited partnership organized under the laws of the State of ___________, whose post office address is:____.

WITNESSETH, that the Grantor, for good consideration and for the sum of ____________ Dollars ($____________) paid by the Grantee, the receipt of which is hereby acknowledged, does hereby transfer, release and quitclaim to Grantee, forever, all right, title, interest and claim which the Grantor has in and to the following described parcel of land, and improvements and appurtenances thereto in the County of ________________, State of ____________, to wit:

IN WITNESS WHEREOF, the Grantor has signed and sealed these presents the day and year first above written. Signed, sealed and delivered in the presence of:

______________________________	______________________________
Witness	Grantor
______________________________	______________________________
Witness	

STATE OF ____________________ §
§
COUNTY OF _________________ §

On this ______ day of ________________, 20_______, before me personally appeared ____________________________, known to me to be the person whose name is subscribed to this Quitclaim Deed and acknowledged to me that he/she executed the same in his/her authorized capacity and that by his/her signature on this Quitclaim Deed the person or entity upon whose behalf the he/she acted, executed the Quitclaim Deed.

____
Notary Public
State of ____________________________
My commission expires:______________

STATE OF ____________________ §
§
COUNTY OF _________________ §

On this ______ day of ________________, 20_______, before me personally appeared ____________________________, known to me to be the person whose name is subscribed to this Quitclaim Deed and acknowledged to me that he/she executed the same in his/her authorized capacity and that by his/her signature on this Quitclaim Deed the person or entity upon whose behalf the he/she acted, executed the Quitclaim Deed.

____
Notary Public
State of ____________________________
My commission expires:______________

Sale of Partnership Interest

AGREEMENT made this ________ day of __________, 20____, by and between _______________, ____________________, and ______________________.

______________________ is a General/Limited Partner in the limited partnership named ______________________________________, a limited partnership organized under the laws of the State of _______________ (the "Partnership"). Pursuant to a Partnership Agreement dated ____________, 20______.

Pursuant to the Partnership Agreement, _________________________ has obtained the approval of the remaining partners to the sale of his/her entire interest in the Partnership.

IT IS THEREFORE AGREED:

1. _________________________ hereby sells and transfers his/her entire partnership interest in the Partnership to _______________________ for the sum of $__________________ payable upon the execution of this Agreement receipt of which is hereby acknowledged.

2. ______________________ agrees to be bound by the terms of the Partnership Agreement dated _____________, 20____, as if he/she had been originally named therein.

IN WITNESS WHEREOF the parties have signed this Agreement on the date first above-written.

____
Selling Partner

____
Purchaser

APPROVED:

__________________________________ __________________________________
General Partner Limited Partner

__________________________________ __________________________________
Limited Partner Limited Partner

This page intentionally left blank.

CHANGE OF REGISTERED AGENT/REGISTERED OFFICE

1. The name of the limited partnership is ______________________ and the file number issued to the limited partnership by the Secretary of State is ______________________.

2. The changes ser forth herein are authorized under the laws of the State of ________________.

3. The registered office of the limited partnership presently shown in the records of the Secretary of State is .

_____ A. The address of the NEW registered office is :________________

or

_____ B. The registered office address will not change

4. The name of the registered agent as presently shown in the records of the Secretary of State is ____________________.

_____ A. The name of the NEW registered agent is ______________________.

or

_____ B. The registered agent will not change.

By: ______________________________
General Partner

This page intentionally left blank.

CERTIFICATE OF WITHDRAWAL

The following is hereby certified:

1. The undersigned, ________________________________, whose address is ________________________, has withdrawn as a limited/general partner from the partnership doing business under the laws of the Sate of ______________ under the name of ______________________________.

2. The partnership has its principal place of business located at: ____________________, ____________________, ____________________, County, State of ____________________.

3. The Assumed/Fictitious name Certificate with respect to the business name was filed in the office of ____________________, State of ____________________, on the ______ day of ____________________, 20____.

Signed this ______ day of ____________________, 20 ______.

ACCEPTED BY:

____________________________	____________________________
General Partner	Withdrawing Partner

STATE OF ________________ §
§
COUNTY OF ______________ §

On this _____ day of ______________, 20______, before me personally appeared ____________________, known to me to be the person whose name is subscribed to this Certificate and acknowledged to me that he/she executed the same in his/her authorized capacity as general partner of ______________________________, and that by his/her signature on this Certificate the person or entity upon whose behalf the he/she acted, executed the Certificate.

____
Notary Public
State of ____________________________
My commission expires:______________

STATE OF ____________________ §
§
COUNTY OF _________________ §

On this ______ day of _______________, 20_______, before me personally appeared ________________________, known to me to be the person whose name is subscribed to this Certificate and acknowledged to me that he/she executed the same in his/her authorized capacity as limited partner of ______________________________, and that by his/her signature on this Certificate the person or entity upon whose behalf the he/she acted, executed the Certificate.

____
Notary Public
State of ____________________________
My commission expires:______________

Form **SS-4**
(Rev. April 2000)
Department of the Treasury
Internal Revenue Service

Application for Employer Identification Number

(For use by employers, corporations, partnerships, trusts, estates, churches, government agencies, certain individuals, and others. See instructions.)

► Keep a copy for your records.

EIN

OMB No. 1545-0003

Please type or print clearly.

1 Name of applicant (legal name) (see instructions)

2 Trade name of business (if different from name on line 1)

3 Executor, trustee, "care of" name

4a Mailing address (street address) (room, apt., or suite no.)

5a Business address (if different from address on lines 4a and 4b)

4b City, state, and ZIP code

5b City, state, and ZIP code

6 County and state where principal business is located

7 Name of principal officer, general partner, grantor, owner, or trustor—SSN or ITIN may be required (see instructions) ► ______

8a Type of entity (Check only one box.) (see instructions)
Caution: *If applicant is a limited liability company, see the instructions for line 8a.*

- ☐ Sole proprietor (SSN) ______
- ☐ Partnership
- ☐ REMIC
- ☐ State/local government
- ☐ Church or church-controlled organization
- ☐ Other nonprofit organization (specify) ► ______ (enter GEN if applicable) ______
- ☐ Other (specify) ►
- ☐ Personal service corp.
- ☐ National Guard
- ☐ Farmers' cooperative
- ☐ Estate (SSN of decedent) ______
- ☐ Plan administrator (SSN) ______
- ☐ Other corporation (specify) ► ______
- ☐ Trust
- ☐ Federal government/military

8b If a corporation, name the state or foreign country (if applicable) where incorporated | State | Foreign country

9 Reason for applying (Check only one box.) (see instructions)

- ☐ Started new business (specify type) ► ______
- ☐ Hired employees (Check the box and see line 12.)
- ☐ Created a pension plan (specify type) ►
- ☐ Banking purpose (specify purpose) ► ______
- ☐ Changed type of organization (specify new type) ► ______
- ☐ Purchased going business
- ☐ Created a trust (specify type) ► ______
- ☐ Other (specify) ►

10 Date business started or acquired (month, day, year) (see instructions)

11 Closing month of accounting year (see instructions)

12 First date wages or annuities were paid or will be paid (month, day, year). **Note:** *If applicant is a withholding agent, enter date income will first be paid to nonresident alien. (month, day, year)* . . . . ►

13 Highest number of employees expected in the next 12 months. **Note:** *If the applicant does not expect to have any employees during the period, enter -0-. (see instructions)* . . . . . ►

Nonagricultural	Agricultural	Household

14 Principal activity (see instructions) ►

15 Is the principal business activity manufacturing? . . . . ☐ **Yes** ☐ **No**
If "Yes," principal product and raw material used ►

16 To whom are most of the products or services sold? Please check one box. ☐ Business (wholesale)
☐ Public (retail) ☐ Other (specify) ► ☐ N/A

17a Has the applicant ever applied for an employer identification number for this or any other business? . . . . ☐ **Yes** ☐ **No**
Note: *If "Yes," please complete lines 17b and 17c.*

17b If you checked "Yes" on line 17a, give applicant's legal name and trade name shown on prior application, if different from line 1 or 2 above.
Legal name ► Trade name ►

17c Approximate date when and city and state where the application was filed. Enter previous employer identification number if known.

Approximate date when filed (mo., day, year)	City and state where filed	Previous EIN

Under penalties of perjury, I declare that I have examined this application, and to the best of my knowledge and belief, it is true, correct, and complete.

Business telephone number (include area code)
( )

Fax telephone number (include area code)
( )

Name and title (Please type or print clearly.) ►

Signature ► Date ►

Note: *Do not write below this line. For official use only.*

Please leave blank ►	Geo.	Ind.	Class	Size	Reason for applying

For Privacy Act and Paperwork Reduction Act Notice, see page 4. Cat. No. 16055N Form **SS-4** (Rev. 4-2000)

Do I Need an EIN?

File Form SS-4 if the applicant entity does not already have an EIN but is required to show an EIN on a
return, statement, or other document.[1] **See also the separate instructions for each line on Form SS-4**

IF the applicant...	AND...	THEN...
Started a new business	Does not currently have (nor expect to have) employees	Complete lines 1, 2, 4a-6, 8a, and
Hired (or will hire) employees, including household employees	Does not already have an EIN	Complete lines 1, 2, 4a-6, 7a-b (if 8a, 8b (if applicable), and 9-16c.
Opened a bank account	Needs an EIN for banking purposes only	Complete lines 1-5b, 7a-b (if appli 9, and 16a-c.
Changed type of organization	Either the legal character of the organization or its ownership changed (e.g., you incorporate a sole proprietorship or form a partnership)[2]	Complete lines 1-16c (as applicabl
Purchased a going business[3]	Does not already have an EIN	Complete lines 1-16c (as applicabl
Created a trust	The trust is other than a grantor trust or an IRA trust[4]	Complete lines 1-16c (as applicabl
Created a pension plan as a plan administrator[5]	Needs an EIN for reporting purposes	Complete lines 1, 2, 4a-6, 8a, 9, a
Is a foreign person needing an EIN to comply with IRS withholding regulations	Needs an EIN to complete a Form W-8 (other than Form W-8ECI), avoid withholding on portfolio assets, or claim tax treaty benefits[6]	Complete lines 1-5b, 7a-b (SSN o optional), 8a-9, and 16a-c.
Is administering an estate	Needs an EIN to report estate income on Form 1041	Complete lines 1, 3, 4a-b, 8a, 9, a
Is a withholding agent for taxes on non-wage income paid to an alien (i.e., individual, corporation, or partnership, etc.)	Is an agent, broker, fiduciary, manager, tenant, or spouse who is required to file **Form 1042,** Annual Withholding Tax Return for U.S. Source Income of Foreign Persons	Complete lines 1, 2, 3 (if applicable 7a-b (if applicable), 8a, 9, and 16a-
Is a state or local agency	Serves as a tax reporting agent for public assistance recipients under Rev. Proc. 80-4, 1980-1 C.B. 581[7]	Complete lines 1, 2, 4a-5b, 8a, 9,
Is a single-member LLC	Needs an EIN to file **Form 8832,** Classification Election, for filing employment tax returns, **or** for state reporting purposes[8]	Complete lines 1-16c (as applicabl
Is an S corporation	Needs an EIN to file **Form 2553,** Election by a Small Business Corporation[9]	Complete lines 1-16c (631-447-4955 bl

[1] For example, a sole proprietorship or self-employed farmer who establishes a qualified retirement plan, or is required to file excise, employment, al or firearms returns, must have an EIN. **A partnership, corporation, REMIC (real estate mortgage investment conduit), nonprofit organization (etc.), or farmers' cooperative must use an EIN for any tax-related purpose even if the entity does not have employees.**

[2] However, **do not** apply for a new EIN if the existing entity only **(a)** changed its business name, **(b)** elected on Form 8832 to change the way it is ta covered by the default rules), or **(c)** terminated its partnership status because at least 50% of the total interests in partnership capit 816-823-7777 w exchanged within a 12-month period. (The EIN of the terminated partnership should continue to be used. See Regulations section 301.6109-1(d)(2)

[3] Do not use the EIN of the prior business unless you became the "owner" of a corporation by acquiring its stock.

[4] However, IRA trusts that are required to file **Form 990-T,** Exempt Organization Business Income Tax Return, must have an EIN.

[5] A plan administrator is the person or group of persons specified as the administrator by the instrument under which the plan is operated.

[6] Entities applying to be a Qualified Intermediary (QI) need a QI-EIN even if they already have an EIN. **See Rev. Proc. 2000-12.**

[7] See also *Household employer* on page 4. (**Note:** State or local agencies may need an EIN for other reasons, e.g., hired employees.)

Kansas, New Mexico, Oklahoma, Texas	Attn: Entity Control Austin, TX 73301 512-460-7843
Alaska, Arizona, California (counties of Alpine, Amador, Butte, Calaveras, Colusa, Contra Costa, Del Norte, El Dorado, Glenn, Humboldt, Lake, Lassen, Marin, Mendocino, Modoc, Napa, Nevada, Placer, Plumas, Sacramento, San Joaquin, Shasta, Sierra, Siskiyou, Solano, Sonoma, Sutter, Tehama, Trinity, Yolo, and Yuba), Colorado, Idaho, Montana, Nebraska, Nevada, North Dakota, Oregon, South Dakota, Utah, Washington, Wyoming	Attn: Entity Control Mail Stop 6271 P.O. Box 9941 Ogden, UT 84201 801-620-7645
California (all other counties), Hawaii	Attn: Entity Control Fresno, CA 93888 559-452-4010
Alabama, Arkansas, Louisiana, Mississippi, North Carolina, Tennessee	Attn: Entity Control Memphis, TN 37501 901-546-3920
If you have no legal residence, principal place of business, or principal office or agency in any state	Attn: Entity Control Philadelphia, PA 19255 215-516-6999

Specific Instructions

The instructions that follow are for those items that are not self-explanatory. Enter N/A (nonapplicable) on the lines that do not apply.

Line 1. Enter the legal name of the entity applying for the EIN exactly as it appears on the social security card, charter, or other applicable legal document.

Individuals. Enter your first name, middle initial, and last name. If you are a sole proprietor, enter your individual name, not your business name. Enter your business name on line 2. Do not use abbreviations or nicknames on line 1.

Trusts. Enter the name of the trust.

Estate of a decedent. Enter the name of the estate.

Partnerships. Enter the legal name of the partnership as it appears in the partnership agreement. **Do not** list the names of the partners on line 1. See the specific instructions for line 7.

Corporations. Enter the corporate name as it appears in the corporation charter or other legal document creating it.

Plan administrators. Enter the name of the plan administrator. A plan administrator who already has an EIN should use that number.

Line 2. Enter the trade name of the business if different from the legal name. The trade name is the "doing business as" name.

Note: *Use the full legal name on line 1 on all tax returns filed for the entity. However, if you enter a trade name on line 2 and choose to use the trade name instead of the legal name, enter the trade name on all returns you file. To prevent processing delays and errors,* ***always*** *use either the legal name only or the trade name only on all tax returns.*

Line 3. Trusts enter the name of the trustee. Estates enter the name of the executor, administrator, or other fiduciary. If the entity applying has a designated person to receive tax information, enter that person's name as the "care of" person. Print or type the first name, middle initial, and last name.

Line 7. Enter the first name, middle initial, last name, and SSN of a principal officer if the business is a corporation; of a general partner if a partnership; of the owner of a single member entity that is disregarded as an entity separate from its owner; or of a grantor, owner, or trustor if a trust. If the person in question is an alien individual with a previously assigned individual taxpayer identification number (ITIN), enter the ITIN in the space provided, instead of an SSN. You are not required to enter an SSN or ITIN if the reason you are applying for an EIN is to make an entity classification election (see Regulations section 301.7701-1 through 301.7701-3), and you are a nonresident alien with no effectively connected income from sources within the United States.

Line 8a. Check the box that best describes the type of entity applying for the EIN. If you are an alien individual with an ITIN previously assigned to you, enter the ITIN in place of a requested SSN.

Caution: *This is not an election for a tax classification of an entity. See "Limited liability company (LLC)" below.*

If not specifically mentioned, check the "Other" box, enter the type of entity and the type of return that will be filed (for example, common trust fund, Form 1065). Do not enter N/A. If you are an alien individual applying for an EIN, see the **Line 7** instructions above.

Sole proprietor. Check this box if you file Schedule C, C-EZ, or F (Form 1040) and have a qualified plan, or are required to file excise, employment, or alcohol, tobacco, or firearms returns, or are a payer of gambling winnings. Enter your SSN (or ITIN) in the space provided. If you are a nonresident alien with are a nonresident alien with no effectively connected income from sources within the United States, you do not need to enter an SSN or ITIN.

REMIC. Check this box if the entity has elected to be treated as a real estate mortgage investment conduit (REMIC). See the Instructions for Form 1066 for more information.

Other nonprofit organization. Check this box if the nonprofit organization is other than a church or church-controlled organization and specify the type of nonprofit organization (for example, an educational organization).

If the organization also seeks tax-exempt status, you must file either **Package 1023,** Application for Recognition of Exemption, or **Package 1024,** Application for Recognition of Exemption Under Section 501(a). Get **Pub. 557,** Tax Exempt Status for Your Organization, for more information.

Group exemption number (GEN). If the organization is covered by a group exemption letter, enter the four-digit GEN. (Do not confuse the GEN with the nine-digit EIN.) If you do not know the GEN, contact the parent organization. Get Pub. 557 for more information about group exemption numbers.

Withholding agent. If you are a withholding agent required to file Form 1042, check the "Other" box and enter "Withholding agent."

Personal service corporation. Check this box if the entity is a personal service corporation. An entity is a personal service corporation for a tax year only if:

- The principal activity of the entity during the testing period (prior tax year) for the tax year is the performance of personal services substantially by employee-owners, and
- The employee-owners own at least 10% of the fair market value of the outstanding stock in the entity on the last day of the testing period.

Personal services include performance of services in such fields as health, law, accounting, or consulting. For more information about personal service corporations, see the **Instructions for Forms 1120 and 1120-A,** and **Pub. 542,** Corporations.

Limited liability company (LLC). See the definition of limited liability company in the **Instructions for Form 1065,** U.S. Partnership Return of Income. An LLC with two or more members can be a partnership or an association taxable as a corporation. An LLC with a single owner can be an association taxable as a corporation or an entity disregarded as an entity separate from its owner. See Form 8832 for more details.

Note: *A domestic LLC with at least two members that does not file Form 8832 is classified as a partnership for Federal income tax purposes.*

- If the entity is classified as a partnership for Federal income tax purposes, check the "partnership" box.
- If the entity is classified as a corporation for Federal income tax purposes, check the "Other corporation" box and write "limited liability co." in the space provided.
- If the entity is disregarded as an entity separate from its owner, check the "Other" box and write in "disregarded entity" in the space provided.

Plan administrator. If the plan administrator is an individual, enter the plan administrator's SSN in the space provided.

Other corporation. This box is for any corporation other than a personal service corporation. If you check this box, enter the type of corporation (such as insurance company) in the space provided.

Household employer. If you are an individual, check the "Other" box and enter "Household employer" and your SSN. If you are a state or local agency serving as a tax reporting agent for public assistance recipients who become household employers, check the "Other" box and enter "Household employer agent." If you are a trust that qualifies as a household employer, you do not need a separate EIN for reporting tax information relating to household employees; use the EIN of the trust.

QSub. For a qualified subchapter S subsidiary (QSub) check the "Other" box and specify "QSub."

Line 9. Check only **one** box. Do not enter N/A.

Started new business. Check this box if you are starting a new business that requires an EIN. If you check this box, enter the type of business being started. **Do not** apply if you already have an EIN and are only adding another place of business.

Hired employees. Check this box if the existing business is requesting an EIN because it has hired or is hiring employees and is therefore required to file employment tax returns. **Do not** apply if you already have an EIN and are only hiring employees. For information on the applicable employment taxes for family members, see **Circular E,** Employer's Tax Guide (Publication 15).

Created a pension plan. Check this box if you have created a pension plan and need an EIN for reporting purposes. Also, enter the type of plan.

Note: *Check this box if you are applying for a trust EIN when a new pension plan is established.*

Banking purpose. Check this box if you are requesting an EIN for banking purposes only, and enter the banking purpose (for example, a bowling league for depositing dues or an investment club for dividend and interest reporting).

Changed type of organization. Check this box if the business is changing its type of organization, for example, if the business was a sole proprietorship and has been incorporated or has become a partnership. If you check this box, specify in the space provided the type of change made, for example, "from sole proprietorship to partnership."

Purchased going business. Check this box if you purchased an existing business. **Do not** use the former owner's EIN. **Do not** apply for a new EIN if you already have one. Use your own EIN.

Created a trust. Check this box if you created a trust, and enter the type of trust created. For example, indicate if the trust is a nonexempt charitable trust or a split-interest trust.

Note: ***Do not*** *check this box if you are applying for a trust EIN when a new pension plan is established. Check "Created a pension plan."*

Exception. Do **not** file this form for certain grantor-type trusts. The trustee does not need an EIN for the trust if the trustee furnishes the name and TIN of the grantor/owner and the address of the trust to all payors. See the Instructions for Form 1041 for more information.

Other (specify). Check this box if you are requesting an EIN for any other reason, and enter the reason.

Line 10. If you are starting a new business, enter the starting date of the business. If the business you acquired is already operating, enter the date you acquired the business. Trusts should enter the date the trust was legally created. Estates should enter the date of death of the decedent whose name appears on line 1 or the date when the estate was legally funded.

Line 11. Enter the last month of your accounting year or tax year. An accounting or tax year is usually 12 consecutive months, either a calendar year or a fiscal year (including a period of 52 or 53 weeks). A calendar year is 12 consecutive months ending on December 31. A fiscal year is either 12 consecutive months ending on the last day of any month other than December or a 52-53 week year. For more information on accounting periods, see **Pub. 538,** Accounting Periods and Methods.

Individuals. Your tax year generally will be a calendar year.

Partnerships. Partnerships generally must adopt one of the following tax years:

- The tax year of the majority of its partners,
- The tax year common to all of its principal partners,
- The tax year that results in the least aggregate deferral of income, or
- In certain cases, some other tax year.

See the Instructions for Form 1065 for more information.

REMIC. REMICs must have a calendar year as their tax year.

Personal service corporations. A personal service corporation generally must adopt a calendar year unless:

- It can establish a business purpose for having a different tax year, or
- It elects under section 444 to have a tax year other than a calendar year.

Trusts. Generally, a trust must adopt a calendar year except for the following:

- Tax-exempt trusts,
- Charitable trusts, and
- Grantor-owned trusts.

Line 12. If the business has or will have employees, enter the date on which the business began or will begin to pay wages. If the business does not plan to have employees, enter N/A.

Withholding agent. Enter the date you began or will begin to pay income to a nonresident alien. This also applies to individuals who are required to file Form 1042 to report alimony paid to a nonresident alien.

Line 13. For a definition of agricultural labor (farmwork), see **Circular A,** Agricultural Employer's Tax Guide (Publication 51).

Line 14. Generally, enter the exact type of business being operated (for example, advertising agency, farm, food or beverage establishment, labor union, real estate agency, steam laundry, rental of coin-operated vending machine, or investment club). Also state if the business will involve the sale or distribution of alcoholic beverages.

Governmental. Enter the type of organization (state, county, school district, municipality, etc.).

Nonprofit organization (other than governmental). Enter whether organized for religious, educational, or humane purposes, and the principal activity (for example, religious organization—hospital, charitable).

Mining and quarrying. Specify the process and the principal product (for example, mining bituminous coal, contract drilling for oil, or quarrying dimension stone).

Contract construction. Specify whether general contracting or special trade contracting. Also, show the type of work normally performed (for example, general contractor for residential buildings or electrical subcontractor).

Food or beverage establishments. Specify the type of establishment and state whether you employ workers who receive tips (for example, lounge—yes).

Trade. Specify the type of sales and the principal line of goods sold (for example, wholesale dairy products, manufacturer's representative for mining machinery, or retail hardware).

Manufacturing. Specify the type of establishment operated (for example, sawmill or vegetable cannery).

Signature. The application must be signed by (a) the individual, if the applicant is an individual, (b) the president, vice president, or other principal officer, if the applicant is a corporation, (c) a responsible and duly authorized member or officer having knowledge of its affairs, if the applicant is a partnership or other unincorporated organization, or (d) the fiduciary, if the applicant is a trust or an estate.

How To Get Forms and Publications

Phone. You can order forms, instructions, and publications by phone 24 hours a day, 7 days a week. Just call 1-800-TAX-FORM (1-800-829-3676). You should receive your order or notification of its status within 10 workdays.

Personal computer. With your personal computer and modem, you can get the forms and information you need using IRS's Internet Web Site at **www.irs.gov** or File Transfer Protocol at **ftp.irs.gov.**

CD-ROM. For small businesses, return preparers, or others who may frequently need tax forms or publications, a CD-ROM containing over 2,000 tax products (including many prior year forms) can be purchased from the National Technical Information Service (NTIS).

To order **Pub. 1796,** Federal Tax Products on CD-ROM, call **1-877-CDFORMS** (1-877-233-6767) toll free or connect to **www.irs.gov/cdorders**

Privacy Act and Paperwork Reduction Act Notice. We ask for the information on this form to carry out the Internal Revenue laws of the United States. We need it to comply with section 6109 and the regulations thereunder which generally require the inclusion of an employer identification number (EIN) on certain returns, statements, or other documents filed with the Internal Revenue Service. Information on this form may be used to determine which Federal tax returns you are required to file and to provide you with related forms and publications. We disclose this form to the Social Security Administration for their use in determining compliance with applicable laws. We will be unable to issue an EIN to you unless you provide all of the requested information which applies to your entity.

You are not required to provide the information requested on a form that is subject to the Paperwork Reduction Act unless the form displays a valid OMB control number. Books or records relating to a form or its instructions must be retained as long as their contents may become material in the administration of any Internal Revenue law. Generally, tax returns/return information are confidential, as required by section 6103.

The time needed to complete and file this form will vary depending on individual circumstances. The estimated average time is:

Recordkeeping	7 min.
Learning about the law or the form	22 min.
Preparing the form	46 min.
Copying, assembling, and sending the form to the IRS	20 min.

If you have comments concerning the accuracy of these time estimates or suggestions for making this form simpler, we would be happy to hear from you. You can write to the Tax Forms Committee, Western Area Distribution Center, Rancho Cordova, CA 95743-0001. **Do not** send the form to this address. Instead, see **Where To Apply** on page 2.

Form **1065**
Department of the Treasury
Internal Revenue Service

U.S. Return of Partnership Income

For calendar year 2001, or tax year beginning ...., 2001, and ending ...., 20....
▶ See separate instructions.

OMB No. 1545-0099

2001

A Principal business activity	Use the IRS label. Otherwise, print or type. Name of partnership	D Employer identification number
B Principal product or service	Number, street, and room or suite no. If a P.O. box, see page 13 of the instructions.	E Date business started
C Business code number	City or town, state, and ZIP code	F Total assets (see page 14 of the instructions) $

G Check applicable boxes: (1) ☐ Initial return (2) ☐ Final return (3) ☐ Name change (4) ☐ Address change (5) ☐ Amended return

H Check accounting method: (1) ☐ Cash (2) ☐ Accrual (3) ☐ Other (specify) ▶

I Number of Schedules K-1. Attach one for each person who was a partner at any time during the tax year ▶

Caution: *Include **only** trade or business income and expenses on lines 1a through 22 below. See the instructions for more information.*

Income	1a Gross receipts or sales	1a			
	b Less returns and allowances	1b		1c	
	2 Cost of goods sold (Schedule A, line 8)			2	
	3 Gross profit. Subtract line 2 from line 1c			3	
	4 Ordinary income (loss) from other partnerships, estates, and trusts *(attach schedule)*			4	
	5 Net farm profit (loss) *(attach Schedule F (Form 1040))*			5	
	6 Net gain (loss) from Form 4797, Part II, line 18			6	
	7 Other income (loss) *(attach schedule)*			7	
	8 **Total income (loss).** Combine lines 3 through 7			8	
Deductions (see page 15 of the instructions for limitations)	9 Salaries and wages (other than to partners) (less employment credits)			9	
	10 Guaranteed payments to partners			10	
	11 Repairs and maintenance			11	
	12 Bad debts			12	
	13 Rent			13	
	14 Taxes and licenses			14	
	15 Interest			15	
	16a Depreciation (if required, attach Form 4562)	16a			
	b Less depreciation reported on Schedule A and elsewhere on return	16b		16c	
	17 Depletion **(Do not deduct oil and gas depletion.)**			17	
	18 Retirement plans, etc.			18	
	19 Employee benefit programs			19	
	20 Other deductions *(attach schedule)*			20	
	21 **Total deductions.** Add the amounts shown in the far right column for lines 9 through 20			21	
	22 **Ordinary income (loss)** from trade or business activities. Subtract line 21 from line 8			22	

Sign Here

Under penalties of perjury, I declare that I have examined this return, including accompanying schedules and statements, and to the best of my knowledge and belief, it is true, correct, and complete. Declaration of preparer (other than general partner or limited liability company member) is based on all information of which preparer has any knowledge.

May the IRS discuss this return with the preparer shown below (see instructions)? ☐ Yes ☐ No

▶ Signature of general partner or limited liability company member ▶ Date

Paid Preparer's Use Only

Preparer's signature	Date	Check if self-employed ▶ ☐	Preparer's SSN or PTIN
Firm's name (or yours if self-employed), address, and ZIP code ▶		EIN ▶	
		Phone no. ( )	

Schedule A Cost of Goods Sold (see page 18 of the instructions)

1	Inventory at beginning of year	1	
2	Purchases less cost of items withdrawn for personal use	2	
3	Cost of labor	3	
4	Additional section 263A costs *(attach schedule)*	4	
5	Other costs *(attach schedule)*	5	
6	**Total.** Add lines 1 through 5	6	
7	Inventory at end of year	7	
8	**Cost of goods sold.** Subtract line 7 from line 6. Enter here and on page 1, line 2	8	

9a Check all methods used for valuing closing inventory:

- **(i)** ☐ Cost as described in Regulations section 1.471-3
- **(ii)** ☐ Lower of cost or market as described in Regulations section 1.471-4
- **(iii)** ☐ Other (specify method used and attach explanation) ▶

b Check this box if there was a writedown of "subnormal" goods as described in Regulations section 1.471-2(c) ▶ ☐

c Check this box if the LIFO inventory method was adopted this tax year for any goods *(if checked, attach Form 970)* ▶ ☐

d Do the rules of section 263A (for property produced or acquired for resale) apply to the partnership? ☐ **Yes** ☐ **No**

e Was there any change in determining quantities, cost, or valuations between opening and closing inventory? ☐ **Yes** ☐ **No**
If "Yes," attach explanation.

Schedule B Other Information

		Yes	No
1	What type of entity is filing this return? Check the applicable box: **a** ☐ Domestic general partnership **b** ☐ Domestic limited partnership **c** ☐ Domestic limited liability company **d** ☐ Domestic limited liability partnership **e** ☐ Foreign partnership **f** ☐ Other ▶		
2	Are any partners in this partnership also partnerships?		
3	During the partnership's tax year, did the partnership own any interest in another partnership or in any foreign entity that was disregarded as an entity separate from its owner under Regulations sections 301.7701-2 and 301.7701-3? If yes, see instructions for required attachment		
4	Is this partnership subject to the consolidated audit procedures of sections 6221 through 6233? If "Yes," see **Designation of Tax Matters Partner** below		
5	Does this partnership meet **all three** of the following requirements? **a** The partnership's total receipts for the tax year were less than $250,000; **b** The partnership's total assets at the end of the tax year were less than $600,000; **and** **c** Schedules K-1 are filed with the return and furnished to the partners on or before the due date (including extensions) for the partnership return. If "Yes," the partnership is not required to complete Schedules L, M-1, and M-2; Item F on page 1 of Form 1065; or Item J on Schedule K-1		
6	Does this partnership have any foreign partners? If "Yes," the partnership may have to file Forms 8804, 8805 and 8813. See page 20 of the instructions		
7	Is this partnership a publicly traded partnership as defined in section 469(k)(2)?		
8	Has this partnership filed, or is it required to file, **Form 8264,** Application for Registration of a Tax Shelter?		
9	At any time during calendar year 2001, did the partnership have an interest in or a signature or other authority over a financial account in a foreign country (such as a bank account, securities account, or other financial account)? See page 20 of the instructions for exceptions and filing requirements for Form TD F 90-22.1. If "Yes," enter the name of the foreign country. ▶		
10	During the tax year, did the partnership receive a distribution from, or was it the grantor of, or transferor to, a foreign trust? If "Yes," the partnership may have to file Form 3520. See page 20 of the instructions		
11	Was there a distribution of property or a transfer (e.g., by sale or death) of a partnership interest during the tax year? If "Yes," you may elect to adjust the basis of the partnership's assets under section 754 by attaching the statement described under **Elections Made By the Partnership** on page 8 of the instructions		
12	Enter the number of Forms 8865 attached to this return ▶		

Designation of Tax Matters Partner (see page 20 of the instructions)

Enter below the general partner designated as the tax matters partner (TMP) for the tax year of this return:

Name of designated TMP ▶

Identifying number of TMP ▶

Address of designated TMP ▶

Schedule K Partners' Shares of Income, Credits, Deductions, etc.

	(a) Distributive share items		(b) Total amount
Income (Loss)	1 Ordinary income (loss) from trade or business activities (page 1, line 22)	1	
	2 Net income (loss) from rental real estate activities *(attach Form 8825)*	2	
	3a Gross income from other rental activities — 3a		
	b Expenses from other rental activities *(attach schedule)* — 3b		
	c Net income (loss) from other rental activities. Subtract line 3b from line 3a	3c	
	4 Portfolio income (loss): a Interest income	4a	
	b Ordinary dividends	4b	
	c Royalty income	4c	
	d Net short-term capital gain (loss) *(attach Schedule D (Form 1065))*	4d	
	e (1) Net long-term capital gain (loss) *(attach Schedule D (Form 1065))*	4e(1)	
	(2) 28% rate gain (loss) ▶ ______ (3) Qualified 5-year gain ▶ ______		
	f Other portfolio income (loss) *(attach schedule)*	4f	
	5 Guaranteed payments to partners	5	
	6 Net section 1231 gain (loss) (other than due to casualty or theft) *(attach Form 4797)*	6	
	7 Other income (loss) *(attach schedule)*	7	
Deductions	8 Charitable contributions *(attach schedule)*	8	
	9 Section 179 expense deduction *(attach Form 4562)*	9	
	10 Deductions related to portfolio income (itemize)	10	
	11 Other deductions *(attach schedule)*	11	
Credits	12a Low-income housing credit:		
	(1) From partnerships to which section 42(j)(5) applies	12a(1)	
	(2) Other than on line 12a(1)	12a(2)	
	b Qualified rehabilitation expenditures related to rental real estate activities *(attach Form 3468)*	12b	
	c Credits (other than credits shown on lines 12a and 12b) related to rental real estate activities	12c	
	d Credits related to other rental activities	12d	
	13 Other credits	13	
Investment Interest	14a Interest expense on investment debts	14a	
	b (1) Investment income included on lines 4a, 4b, 4c, and 4f above	14b(1)	
	(2) Investment expenses included on line 10 above	14b(2)	
Self-Employment	15a Net earnings (loss) from self-employment	15a	
	b Gross farming or fishing income	15b	
	c Gross nonfarm income	15c	
Adjustments and Tax Preference Items	16a Depreciation adjustment on property placed in service after 1986	16a	
	b Adjusted gain or loss	16b	
	c Depletion (other than oil and gas)	16c	
	d (1) Gross income from oil, gas, and geothermal properties	16d(1)	
	(2) Deductions allocable to oil, gas, and geothermal properties	16d(2)	
	e Other adjustments and tax preference items *(attach schedule)*	16e	
Foreign Taxes	17a Name of foreign country or U.S. possession ▶ ______		
	b Gross income from all sources	17b	
	c Gross income sourced at partner level	17c	
	d Foreign gross income sourced at partnership level:		
	(1) Passive ▶ ______ (2) Listed categories *(attach schedule)* ▶ ______ (3) General limitation ▶	17d(3)	
	e Deductions allocated and apportioned at partner level:		
	(1) Interest expense ▶ ______ (2) Other ▶	17e(2)	
	f Deductions allocated and apportioned at partnership level to foreign source income:		
	(1) Passive ▶ ______ (2) Listed categories *(attach schedule)* ▶ ______ (3) General limitation ▶	17f(3)	
	g Total foreign taxes (check one): ▶ Paid ☐ Accrued ☐	17g	
	h Reduction in taxes available for credit *(attach schedule)*	17h	
Other	18 Section 59(e)(2) expenditures: a Type ▶ ______ b Amount ▶	18b	
	19 Tax-exempt interest income	19	
	20 Other tax-exempt income	20	
	21 Nondeductible expenses	21	
	22 Distributions of money (cash and marketable securities)	22	
	23 Distributions of property other than money	23	
	24 Other items and amounts required to be reported separately to partners *(attach schedule)*		

Analysis of Net Income (Loss)

1	Net income (loss). Combine Schedule K, lines 1 through 7 in column (b). From the result, subtract the sum of Schedule K, lines 8 through 11, 14a, 17g, and 18b . . .	1	

2 Analysis by partner type:	(i) Corporate	(ii) Individual (active)	(iii) Individual (passive)	(iv) Partnership	(v) Exempt organization	(vi) Nominee/Other
a General partners						
b Limited partners						

Schedule L — Balance Sheets per Books (Not required if Question 5 on Schedule B is answered "Yes.")

Assets	Beginning of tax year (a)	Beginning of tax year (b)	End of tax year (c)	End of tax year (d)
1 Cash . . .				
2a Trade notes and accounts receivable . . .				
b Less allowance for bad debts . . .				
3 Inventories . . .				
4 U.S. government obligations . . .				
5 Tax-exempt securities . . .				
6 Other current assets *(attach schedule)* . . .				
7 Mortgage and real estate loans . . .				
8 Other investments *(attach schedule)* . . .				
9a Buildings and other depreciable assets . . .				
b Less accumulated depreciation . . .				
10a Depletable assets . . .				
b Less accumulated depletion . . .				
11 Land (net of any amortization) . . .				
12a Intangible assets (amortizable only) . . .				
b Less accumulated amortization . . .				
13 Other assets *(attach schedule)* . . .				
14 **Total** assets . . .				
Liabilities and Capital				
15 Accounts payable . . .				
16 Mortgages, notes, bonds payable in less than 1 year				
17 Other current liabilities *(attach schedule)* . . .				
18 All nonrecourse loans . . .				
19 Mortgages, notes, bonds payable in 1 year or more				
20 Other liabilities *(attach schedule)* . . .				
21 Partners' capital accounts . . .				
22 **Total** liabilities and capital . . .				

Schedule M-1 — Reconciliation of Income (Loss) per Books With Income (Loss) per Return (Not required if Question 5 on Schedule B is answered "Yes.")

1 Net income (loss) per books . . .		6 Income recorded on books this year not included on Schedule K, lines 1 through 7 (itemize): a Tax-exempt interest $	
2 Income included on Schedule K, lines 1 through 4, 6, and 7, not recorded on books this year (itemize):		7 Deductions included on Schedule K, lines 1 through 11, 14a, 17g, and 18b, not charged against book income this year (itemize): a Depreciation $	
3 Guaranteed payments (other than health insurance) . . .		8 Add lines 6 and 7 . . .	
4 Expenses recorded on books this year not included on Schedule K, lines 1 through 11, 14a, 17g, and 18b (itemize): a Depreciation $ .... b Travel and entertainment $		9 Income (loss) (Analysis of Net Income (Loss), line 1). Subtract line 8 from line 5 . . .	
5 Add lines 1 through 4 . . .			

Schedule M-2 — Analysis of Partners' Capital Accounts (Not required if Question 5 on Schedule B is answered "Yes.")

1 Balance at beginning of year . . .		6 Distributions: a Cash . . .	
2 Capital contributed during year . . .		b Property . . .	
3 Net income (loss) per books . . .		7 Other decreases (itemize):	
4 Other increases (itemize):		8 Add lines 6 and 7 . . .	
5 Add lines 1 through 4 . . .		9 Balance at end of year. Subtract line 8 from line 5	

SCHEDULE K-1 (Form 1065)
Department of the Treasury
Internal Revenue Service

Partner's Share of Income, Credits, Deductions, etc.

▶ See separate instructions.

For calendar year 2001 or tax year beginning , 2001, and ending , 20

OMB No. 1545-0099

2001

Partner's identifying number ▶

Partner's name, address, and ZIP code

Partnership's identifying number ▶

Partnership's name, address, and ZIP code

A This partner is a ☐ general partner ☐ limited partner ☐ limited liability company member
B What type of entity is this partner? ▶ ____________
C Is this partner a ☐ domestic or a ☐ foreign partner?

D Enter partner's percentage of:

	(i) Before change or termination	(ii) End of year
Profit sharing	%	%
Loss sharing	%	%
Ownership of capital	%	%

E IRS Center where partnership filed return:

F Partner's share of liabilities (see instructions):
Nonrecourse . . . . $ ____________
Qualified nonrecourse financing . . $ ____________
Other . . . . $ ____________

G Tax shelter registration number . . ▶ ____________

H Check here if this partnership is a publicly traded partnership as defined in section 469(k)(2) . . . . . . ☐

I Check applicable boxes: (1) ☐ Final K-1 (2) ☐ Amended K-1

J Analysis of partner's capital account:

(a) Capital account at beginning of year	(b) Capital contributed during year	(c) Partner's share of lines 3, 4, and 7, Form 1065, Schedule M-2	(d) Withdrawals and distributions	(e) Capital account at end of year (combine columns (a) through (d))
			( )	

	(a) Distributive share item		(b) Amount	(c) 1040 filers enter the amount in column (b) on:
Income (Loss)	1 Ordinary income (loss) from trade or business activities . . .	1		See page 6 of Partner's Instructions for Schedule K-1 (Form 1065).
	2 Net income (loss) from rental real estate activities	2		
	3 Net income (loss) from other rental activities	3		
	4 Portfolio income (loss):			
	a Interest	4a		Sch. B, Part I, line 1
	b Ordinary dividends	4b		Sch. B, Part II, line 5
	c Royalties	4c		Sch. E, Part I, line 4
	d Net short-term capital gain (loss)	4d		Sch. D, line 5, col. (f)
	e (1) Net long-term capital gain (loss).	4e(1)		Sch. D, line 12, col. (f)
	(2) 28% rate gain (loss)	4e(2)		Sch. D, line 12, col. (g)
	(3) Qualified 5-year gain	4e(3)		Line 4 of worksheet for Sch. D, line 29
	f Other portfolio income (loss) *(attach schedule)*	4f		Enter on applicable line of your return.
	5 Guaranteed payments to partner	5		See page 6 of Partner's Instructions for Schedule K-1 (Form 1065).
	6 Net section 1231 gain (loss) (other than due to casualty or theft)	6		
	7 Other income (loss) *(attach schedule)*	7		Enter on applicable line of your return.
Deductions	8 Charitable contributions (see instructions) *(attach schedule)* . .	8		Sch. A, line 15 or 16
	9 Section 179 expense deduction	9		See pages 7 and 8 of Partner's Instructions for Schedule K-1 (Form 1065).
	10 Deductions related to portfolio income *(attach schedule)* . . .	10		
	11 Other deductions *(attach schedule)*.	11		
Credits	12a Low-income housing credit:			
	(1) From section 42(j)(5) partnerships	12a(1)		Form 8586, line 5
	(2) Other than on line 12a(1)	12a(2)		
	b Qualified rehabilitation expenditures related to rental real estate activities	12b		See page 8 of Partner's Instructions for Schedule K-1 (Form 1065).
	c Credits (other than credits shown on lines 12a and 12b) related to rental real estate activities.	12c		
	d Credits related to other rental activities	12d		
	13 Other credits.	13		

For Paperwork Reduction Act Notice, see Instructions for Form 1065. Cat. No. 11394R **Schedule K-1 (Form 1065) 2001**

	(a) Distributive share item		(b) Amount	(c) 1040 filers enter the amount in column (b) on:
Investment Interest	**14a** Interest expense on investment debts	14a		Form 4952, line 1
	b (1) Investment income included on lines 4a, 4b, 4c, and 4f	14b(1)		See page 9 of Partner's Instructions for Schedule K-1 (Form 1065).
	(2) Investment expenses included on line 10	14b(2)		
Self-employment	**15a** Net earnings (loss) from self-employment	15a		Sch. SE, Section A or B
	b Gross farming or fishing income	15b		See page 9 of Partner's Instructions for Schedule K-1 (Form 1065).
	c Gross nonfarm income	15c		
Adjustments and Tax Preference Items	**16a** Depreciation adjustment on property placed in service after 1986	16a		See page 9 of Partner's Instructions for Schedule K-1 (Form 1065) and Instructions for Form 6251.
	b Adjusted gain or loss	16b		
	c Depletion (other than oil and gas)	16c		
	d (1) Gross income from oil, gas, and geothermal properties	16d(1)		
	(2) Deductions allocable to oil, gas, and geothermal properties	16d(2)		
	e Other adjustments and tax preference items *(attach schedule)*	16e		
Foreign Taxes	**17a** Name of foreign country or U.S. possession ▶			Form 1116, Part I
	b Gross income from all sources	17b		
	c Gross income sourced at partner level	17c		
	d Foreign gross income sourced at partnership level:			
	(1) Passive	17d(1)		
	(2) Listed categories *(attach schedule)*	17d(2)		
	(3) General limitation	17d(3)		
	e Deductions allocated and apportioned at partner level:			
	(1) Interest expense	17e(1)		
	(2) Other	17e(2)		
	f Deductions allocated and apportioned at partnership level to foreign source income:			
	(1) Passive	17f(1)		
	(2) Listed categories *(attach schedule)*	17f(2)		
	(3) General limitation	17f(3)		
	g Total foreign taxes (check one): ▶ ☐ Paid ☐ Accrued	17g		Form 1116, Part II
	h Reduction in taxes available for credit *(attach schedule)*	17h		Form 1116, line 12
Other	**18** Section 59(e)(2) expenditures: **a** Type ▶			See page 9 of Partner's Instructions for Schedule K-1 (Form 1065).
	b Amount	18b		
	19 Tax-exempt interest income	19		Form 1040, line 8b
	20 Other tax-exempt income	20		See pages 9 and 10 of Partner's Instructions for Schedule K-1 (Form 1065).
	21 Nondeductible expenses	21		
	22 Distributions of money (cash and marketable securities)	22		
	23 Distributions of property other than money	23		
	24 Recapture of low-income housing credit:			
	a From section 42(j)(5) partnerships	24a		Form 8611, line 8
	b Other than on line 24a	24b		

Supplemental Information

25 Supplemental information required to be reported separately to each partner *(attach additional schedules if more space is needed)*:

Form 1040 Department of the Treasury—Internal Revenue Service U.S. Individual Income Tax Return 2001

(99) IRS Use Only—Do not write or staple in this space.

For the year Jan. 1–Dec. 31, 2001, or other tax year beginning , 2001, ending , 20

OMB No. 1545-0074

Label

(See instructions on page 19.)

Use the IRS label. Otherwise, please print or type.

LABEL HERE

Your first name and initial	Last name	Your social security number
If a joint return, spouse's first name and initial	Last name	Spouse's social security number
Home address (number and street). If you have a P.O. box, see page 19.	Apt. no.	
City, town or post office, state, and ZIP code. If you have a foreign address, see page 19.		

▲ **Important!** ▲ You **must** enter your SSN(s) above.

Presidential Election Campaign (See page 19.)

Note. Checking "Yes" will not change your tax or reduce your refund.
Do you, or your spouse if filing a joint return, want $3 to go to this fund? ▶

You ☐ Yes ☐ No Spouse ☐ Yes ☐ No

Filing Status

Check only one box.

1 ☐ Single
2 ☐ Married filing joint return (even if only one had income)
3 ☐ Married filing separate return. Enter spouse's social security no. above and full name here. ▶
4 ☐ Head of household (with qualifying person). (See page 19.) If the qualifying person is a child but not your dependent, enter this child's name here. ▶
5 ☐ Qualifying widow(er) with dependent child (year spouse died ▶). (See page 19.)

Exemptions

6a ☐ **Yourself.** If your parent (or someone else) can claim you as a dependent on his or her tax return, **do not** check box 6a

b ☐ **Spouse**

c **Dependents:**

If more than six dependents, see page 20.

(1) First name Last name	(2) Dependent's social security number	(3) Dependent's relationship to you	(4) ✓ if qualifying child for child tax credit (see page 20)
			☐
			☐
			☐
			☐
			☐
			☐

d Total number of exemptions claimed

No. of boxes checked on 6a and 6b
No. of your children on 6c who:
• lived with you
• did not live with you due to divorce or separation (see page 20)
Dependents on 6c not entered above
Add numbers entered on lines above ▶

Income

Attach Forms W-2 and W-2G here. Also attach Form(s) 1099-R if tax was withheld.

If you did not get a W-2, see page 21.

Enclose, but do not attach, any payment. Also, please use Form 1040-V.

7	Wages, salaries, tips, etc. Attach Form(s) W-2		7
8a	**Taxable** interest. Attach Schedule B if required		8a
b	**Tax-exempt** interest. **Do not** include on line 8a	8b	
9	Ordinary dividends. Attach Schedule B if required		9
10	Taxable refunds, credits, or offsets of state and local income taxes (see page 22)		10
11	Alimony received		11
12	Business income or (loss). Attach Schedule C or C-EZ		12
13	Capital gain or (loss). Attach Schedule D if required. If not required, check here ▶ ☐		13
14	Other gains or (losses). Attach Form 4797		14
15a	Total IRA distributions	15a	b Taxable amount (see page 23) 15b
16a	Total pensions and annuities	16a	b Taxable amount (see page 23) 16b
17	Rental real estate, royalties, partnerships, S corporations, trusts, etc. Attach Schedule E		17
18	Farm income or (loss). Attach Schedule F		18
19	Unemployment compensation		19
20a	Social security benefits	20a	b Taxable amount (see page 25) 20b
21	Other income. List type and amount (see page 27)		21
22	Add the amounts in the far right column for lines 7 through 21. This is your **total income** ▶		22

Adjusted Gross Income

23	IRA deduction (see page 27)	23	
24	Student loan interest deduction (see page 28)	24	
25	Archer MSA deduction. Attach Form 8853	25	
26	Moving expenses. Attach Form 3903	26	
27	One-half of self-employment tax. Attach Schedule SE	27	
28	Self-employed health insurance deduction (see page 30)	28	
29	Self-employed SEP, SIMPLE, and qualified plans	29	
30	Penalty on early withdrawal of savings	30	
31a	Alimony paid b Recipient's SSN ▶	31a	
32	Add lines 23 through 31a		32
33	Subtract line 32 from line 22. This is your **adjusted gross income** ▶		33

Tax and Credits

Standard Deduction for-

- People who checked any box on line 35a or 35b **or** who can be claimed as a dependent, see page 31.
- All others:

Single, $4,550

Head of household, $6,650

Married filing jointly or Qualifying widow(er), $7,600

Married filing separately, $3,800

34	Amount from line 33 (adjusted gross income)	34	
35a	Check if: ☐ **You** were 65 or older, ☐ Blind; ☐ **Spouse** was 65 or older, ☐ Blind. Add the number of boxes checked above and enter the total here ▶ 35a		
b	If you are married filing separately and your spouse itemizes deductions, or you were a dual-status alien, see page 31 and check here ▶ 35b ☐		
36	**Itemized deductions** (from Schedule A) **or** your **standard deduction** (see left margin)	36	
37	Subtract line 36 from line 34	37	
38	If line 34 is $99,725 or less, multiply $2,900 by the total number of exemptions claimed on line 6d. If line 34 is over $99,725, see the worksheet on page 32	38	
39	**Taxable income.** Subtract line 38 from line 37. If line 38 is more than line 37, enter -0-	39	
40	**Tax** (see page 33). Check if any tax is from **a** ☐ Form(s) 8814 **b** ☐ Form 4972	40	
41	**Alternative minimum tax** (see page 34). Attach Form 6251	41	
42	Add lines 40 and 41 ▶	42	
43	Foreign tax credit. Attach Form 1116 if required — 43		
44	Credit for child and dependent care expenses. Attach Form 2441 — 44		
45	Credit for the elderly or the disabled. Attach Schedule R — 45		
46	Education credits. Attach Form 8863 — 46		
47	Rate reduction credit. See the worksheet on page 36 — 47		
48	Child tax credit (see page 37) — 48		
49	Adoption credit. Attach Form 8839 — 49		
50	Other credits from: **a** ☐ Form 3800 **b** ☐ Form 8396 **c** ☐ Form 8801 **d** ☐ Form (specify) ______ — 50		
51	Add lines 43 through 50. These are your **total credits**	51	
52	Subtract line 51 from line 42. If line 51 is more than line 42, enter -0- ▶	52	

Other Taxes

53	Self-employment tax. Attach Schedule SE	53	
54	Social security and Medicare tax on tip income not reported to employer. Attach Form 4137	54	
55	Tax on qualified plans, including IRAs, and other tax-favored accounts. Attach Form 5329 if required	55	
56	Advance earned income credit payments from Form(s) W-2	56	
57	Household employment taxes. Attach Schedule H	57	
58	Add lines 52 through 57. This is your **total tax** ▶	58	

Payments

If you have a qualifying child, attach Schedule EIC.

59	Federal income tax withheld from Forms W-2 and 1099 — 59		
60	2001 estimated tax payments and amount applied from 2000 return — 60		
61a	**Earned income credit (EIC)** — 61a		
b	Nontaxable earned income — 61b		
62	Excess social security and RRTA tax withheld (see page 51) — 62		
63	Additional child tax credit. Attach Form 8812 — 63		
64	Amount paid with request for extension to file (see page 51) — 64		
65	Other payments. Check if from **a** ☐ Form 2439 **b** ☐ Form 4136 — 65		
66	Add lines 59, 60, 61a, and 62 through 65. These are your **total payments** ▶	66	

Refund

Direct deposit? See page 51 and fill in 68b, 68c, and 68d.

67	If line 66 is more than line 58, subtract line 58 from line 66. This is the amount you **overpaid**	67	
68a	Amount of line 67 you want **refunded to you** ▶	68a	
▶ b	Routing number ☐☐☐☐☐☐☐☐☐ ▶ **c** Type: ☐ Checking ☐ Savings		
▶ d	Account number ☐☐☐☐☐☐☐☐☐☐☐☐☐☐☐☐☐		
69	Amount of line 67 you want **applied to your 2002 estimated tax** ▶ 69		

Amount You Owe

70	**Amount you owe.** Subtract line 66 from line 58. For details on how to pay, see page 52 ▶	70	
71	Estimated tax penalty. Also include on line 70 — 71		

Third Party Designee

Do you want to allow another person to discuss this return with the IRS (see page 53)? ☐ **Yes.** Complete the following. ☐ **No**

Designee's name ▶ Phone no. ▶ ( ) Personal identification number (PIN) ▶ ☐☐☐☐☐

Sign Here

Joint return? See page 19. Keep a copy for your records.

Under penalties of perjury, I declare that I have examined this return and accompanying schedules and statements, and to the best of my knowledge and belief, they are true, correct, and complete. Declaration of preparer (other than taxpayer) is based on all information of which preparer has any knowledge.

Your signature	Date	Your occupation	Daytime phone number ( )
Spouse's signature. If a joint return, **both** must sign.	Date	Spouse's occupation	

Paid Preparer's Use Only

Preparer's signature ▶	Date	Check if self-employed ☐	Preparer's SSN or PTIN
Firm's name (or yours if self-employed), address, and ZIP code ▶		EIN	
		Phone no. ( )	

SCHEDULE E (Form 1040)

Department of the Treasury Internal Revenue Service (99)

Supplemental Income and Loss

(From rental real estate, royalties, partnerships, S corporations, estates, trusts, REMICs, etc.)

▶ Attach to Form 1040 or Form 1041. ▶ See Instructions for Schedule E (Form 1040).

OMB No. 1545-0074

2001

Attachment Sequence No. 13

Name(s) shown on return | **Your social security number**

Part I **Income or Loss From Rental Real Estate and Royalties** **Note.** If you are in the business of renting personal property, use **Schedule C** or **C-EZ** (see page E-1). Report farm rental income or loss from **Form 4835** on page 2, line 39.

1	Show the kind and location of each **rental real estate property:**
A	
B	
C	

2 For each rental real estate property listed on line 1, did you or your family use it during the tax year for personal purposes for more than the greater of:
- 14 days **or**
- 10% of the total days rented at fair rental value?

(See page E-1.)

	Yes	No
A		
B		
C		

		Properties A	Properties B	Properties C		Totals (Add columns A, B, and C.)
Income:						
3 Rents received	3				3	
4 Royalties received	4				4	
Expenses:						
5 Advertising	5					
6 Auto and travel (see page E-2)	6					
7 Cleaning and maintenance	7					
8 Commissions	8					
9 Insurance	9					
10 Legal and other professional fees	10					
11 Management fees	11					
12 Mortgage interest paid to banks, etc. (see page E-2)	12				12	
13 Other interest	13					
14 Repairs	14					
15 Supplies	15					
16 Taxes	16					
17 Utilities	17					
18 Other (list) ▶	18					
19 Add lines 5 through 18	19				19	
20 Depreciation expense or depletion (see page E-3)	20				20	
21 Total expenses. Add lines 19 and 20	21					
22 Income or (loss) from rental real estate or royalty properties. Subtract line 21 from line 3 (rents) or line 4 (royalties). If the result is a (loss), see page E-3 to find out if you must file **Form 6198**	22					
23 Deductible rental real estate loss. **Caution.** Your rental real estate loss on line 22 may be limited. See page E-3 to find out if you must file **Form 8582.** Real estate professionals must complete line 42 on page 2	23	( )	( )	( )		

24 **Income.** Add positive amounts shown on line 22. **Do not** include any losses	24	
25 **Losses.** Add royalty losses from line 22 and rental real estate losses from line 23. Enter total losses here	25	( )
26 **Total rental real estate and royalty income or (loss).** Combine lines 24 and 25. Enter the result here. If Parts II, III, IV, and line 39 on page 2 do not apply to you, also enter this amount on Form 1040, line 17. Otherwise, include this amount in the total on line 40 on page 2	26	

Name(s) shown on return. Do not enter name and social security number if shown on other side. | **Your social security number**

Note. If you report amounts from farming or fishing on Schedule E, you must enter your gross income from those activities on line 41 below. Real estate professionals must complete line 42 below.

Part II Income or Loss From Partnerships and S Corporations

Note. If you report a loss from an at-risk activity, you **must** check either column **(e)** or **(f)** on line 27 to describe your investment in the activity. See page E-5. If you check column **(f)**, you must attach **Form 6198.**

27	(a) Name	(b) Enter P for partnership; S for S corporation	(c) Check if foreign partnership	(d) Employer identification number	Investment At Risk? (e) All is at risk	(f) Some is not at risk
A						
B						
C						
D						
E						

	Passive Income and Loss		Nonpassive Income and Loss		
	(g) Passive loss allowed (attach **Form 8582** if required)	(h) Passive income from **Schedule K-1**	(i) Nonpassive loss from **Schedule K-1**	(j) Section 179 expense deduction from **Form 4562**	(k) Nonpassive income from **Schedule K-1**
A					
B					
C					
D					
E					
28a Totals					
b Totals					

29	Add columns (h) and (k) of line 28a	29	
30	Add columns (g), (i), and (j) of line 28b	30	( )
31	Total partnership and S corporation income or (loss). Combine lines 29 and 30. Enter the result here and include in the total on line 40 below	31	

Part III Income or Loss From Estates and Trusts

32	(a) Name	(b) Employer identification number
A		
B		

	Passive Income and Loss		Nonpassive Income and Loss	
	(c) Passive deduction or loss allowed (attach **Form 8582** if required)	(d) Passive income from **Schedule K-1**	(e) Deduction or loss from **Schedule K-1**	(f) Other income from **Schedule K-1**
A				
B				
33a Totals				
b Totals				

34	Add columns (d) and (f) of line 33a	34	
35	Add columns (c) and (e) of line 33b	35	( )
36	Total estate and trust income or (loss). Combine lines 34 and 35. Enter the result here and include in the total on line 40 below	36	

Part IV Income or Loss From Real Estate Mortgage Investment Conduits (REMICs)- Residual Holder

37 (a) Name	(b) Employer identification number	(c) Excess inclusion from **Schedules Q,** line 2c (see page E-6)	(d) Taxable income (net loss) from **Schedules Q,** line 1b	(e) Income from **Schedules Q,** line 3b

38	Combine columns (d) and (e) only. Enter the result here and include in the total on line 40 below	38	

Part V Summary

39	Net farm rental income or (loss) from **Form 4835**. Also, complete line 41 below	39	
40	**Total** income or (loss). Combine lines 26, 31, 36, 38, and 39. Enter the result here and on Form 1040, line 17 ▶	40	
41	**Reconciliation of Farming and Fishing Income.** Enter your **gross** farming and fishing income reported on Form 4835, line 7; Schedule K-1 (Form 1065), line 15b; Schedule K-1 (Form 1120S), line 23; and Schedule K-1 (Form 1041), line 14 (see page E-6)	41	
42	**Reconciliation for Real Estate Professionals.** If you were a real estate professional (see page E-4), enter the net income or (loss) you reported anywhere on Form 1040 from all rental real estate activities in which you materially participated under the passive activity loss rules	42	

Index

A

B

C

D

P

Q

R

S

T

U

V

W

Sphinx® Publishing's National Titles

Valid in All 50 States

Legal Survival in Business

The Complete Book of Corporate Forms	$24.95
The Complete Patent Book	$26.95
The Entrepreneur's Internet Handbook	$21.95
How to Form a Limited Liability Company	$22.95
Incorporate in Delaware from Any State	$24.95
Incorporate in Nevada from Any State	$24.95
How to Form a Nonprofit Corporation (2E)	$24.95
How to Form Your Own Corporation (3E)	$24.95
How to Form Your Own Partnership (2E)	$24.95
How to Register Your Own Copyright (4E)	$24.95
How to Register Your Own Trademark (3E)	$21.95
Most Valuable Business Legal Forms You'll Ever Need (3E)	$21.95
The Small Business Owner's Guide to Bankruptcy	$21.95

Legal Survival in Court

Crime Victim's Guide to Justice (2E)	$21.95
Grandparents' Rights (3E)	$24.95
Help Your Lawyer Win Your Case (2E)	$14.95
Jurors' Rights (2E)	$12.95
Legal Research Made Easy (3E)	$21.95
Winning Your Personal Injury Claim (2E)	$24.95
Your Rights When You Owe Too Much	$16.95

Legal Survival in Real Estate

Essential Guide to Real Estate Contracts	$18.95
Essential Guide to Real Estate Leases	$18.95
How to Buy a Condominium or Townhome (2E)	$19.95

Legal Survival in Personal Affairs

Cómo Hacer su Propio Testamento	$16.95
Cómo Solicitar su Propio Divorcio	$24.95
Cómo Restablecer su propio Crédito y Renegociar sus Deudas	$21.95
Family Limited Partnership	$26.95
Guía de Inmigración a Estados Unidos (3E)	$24.95
Guía de Justicia para Víctimas del Crimen	$21.95
The 529 College Savings Plan	$16.95
The Complete Legal Guide to Senior Care	$21.95
How to File Your Own Bankruptcy (5E)	$21.95
How to File Your Own Divorce (4E)	$24.95
How to Make Your Own Simple Will (3E)	$18.95
How to Write Your Own Living Will (3E)	$18.95
How to Write Your Own Premarital Agreement (3E)	$24.95
Inmigración a los EE. UU. Paso a Paso	$22.95
Living Trusts and Other Ways to Avoid Probate (3E)	$24.95
Manual de Beneficios para el Seguro Social	$18.95
Mastering the MBE	$16.95
Most Valuable Personal Legal Forms You'll Ever Need	$24.95
Neighbor v. Neighbor (2E)	$16.95
The Nanny and Domestic Help Legal Kit	$22.95
The Power of Attorney Handbook (4E)	$19.95
Repair Your Own Credit and Deal with Debt	$18.95
The Social Security Benefits Handbook (3E)	$18.95
Social Security Q&A	$12.95
Sexual Harassment:Your Guide to Legal Action	$18.95
Teen Rights	$22.95
Unmarried Parents' Rights (2E)	$19.95
U.S. Immigration Step by Step	$21.95
U.S.A. Immigration Guide (4E)	$24.95
The Visitation Handbook	$18.95
Win Your Unemployment Compensation Claim (2E)	$21.95
Your Right to Child Custody, Visitation and Support (2E)	$24.95

Legal Survival Guides are directly available from Sourcebooks, Inc., or from your local bookstores.
Prices are subject to change without notice.
For credit card orders call 1–800–432–7444, write P.O. Box 4410, Naperville, IL 60567-4410
or fax 630-961-2168

SPHINX® PUBLISHING ORDER FORM

BILL TO:		SHIP TO:	
Phone #	Terms	F.O.B. Chicago, IL	Ship Date

Charge my: ❒ VISA ❒ MasterCard ❒ American Express

❒ **Money Order or Personal Check**

Credit Card Number

Expiration Date

Qty	ISBN	Title	Retail	Ext.
		SPHINX PUBLISHING NATIONAL TITLES		
____	1-57248-148-X	Cómo Hacer su Propio Testamento	$16.95	____
____	1-57248-226-5	Cómo Restablecer su propio Crédito y Renegociar sus Deudas	$21.95	____
____	1-57248-147-1	Cómo Solicitar su Propio Divorcio	$24.95	____
____	1-57248-238-9	The 529 College Savings Plan	$16.95	____
____	1-57248-166-8	The Complete Book of Corporate Forms	$24.95	____
____	1-57248-229-X	The Complete Legal Guide to Senior Care	$21.95	____
____	1-57248-201-X	The Complete Patent Book	$26.95	____
____	1-57248-163-3	Crime Victim's Guide to Justice (2E)	$21.95	____
____	1-57248-251-6	The Entrepreneur's Internet Handbook	$21.95	____
____	1-57248-159-5	Essential Guide to Real Estate Contracts	$18.95	____
____	1-57248-160-9	Essential Guide to Real Estate Leases	$18.95	____
____	1-57248-254-0	Family Limited Partnership	$26.95	____
____	1-57248-139-0	Grandparents' Rights (3E)	$24.95	____
____	1-57248-188-9	Guía de Inmigración a Estados Unidos (3E)	$24.95	____
____	1-57248-187-0	Guía de Justicia para Víctimas del Crimen	$21.95	____
____	1-57248-103-X	Help Your Lawyer Win Your Case (2E)	$14.95	____
____	1-57248-164-1	How to Buy a Condominium or Townhome (2E)	$19.95	____
____	1-57248-191-9	How to File Your Own Bankruptcy (5E)	$21.95	____
____	1-57248-132-3	How to File Your Own Divorce (4E)	$24.95	____
____	1-57248-083-1	How to Form a Limited Liability Company	$22.95	____
____	1-57248-231-1	How to Form a Nonprofit Corporation (2E)	$24.95	____
____	1-57248-133-1	How to Form Your Own Corporation (3E)	$24.95	____
____	1-57248-224-9	How to Form Your Own Partnership (2E)	$24.95	____
____	1-57248-232-X	How to Make Your Own Simple Will (3E)	$18.95	____
____	1-57248-200-1	How to Register Your Own Copyright (4E)	$24.95	____
____	1-57248-104-8	How to Register Your Own Trademark (3E)	$21.95	____
____	1-57248-233-8	How to Write Your Own Living Will (3E)	$18.95	____
____	1-57248-156-0	How to Write Your Own Premarital Agreement (3E)	$24.95	____
____	1-57248-230-3	Incorporate in Delaware from Any State	$24.95	____
____	1-57248-158-7	Incorporate in Nevada from Any State	$24.95	____
____	1-57248-250-8	Inmigración a los EE.UU. Paso a Paso	$22.95	____
____	1-57071-333-2	Jurors' Rights (2E)	$12.95	____
____	1-57248-223-0	Legal Research Made Easy (3E)	$21.95	____
____	1-57248-165-X	Living Trusts and Other Ways to Avoid Probate (3E)	$24.95	____

Qty	ISBN	Title	Retail	Ext.
____	1-57248-186-2	Manual de Beneficios para el Seguro Social	$18.95	____
____	1-57248-220-6	Mastering the MBE	$16.95	____
____	1-57248-167-6	Most Valuable Bus. Legal Forms You'll Ever Need (3E)	$21.95	____
____	1-57248-130-7	Most Valuable Personal Legal Forms You'll Ever Need	$24.95	____
____	1-57248-098-X	The Nanny and Domestic Help Legal Kit	$22.95	____
____	1-57248-089-0	Neighbor v. Neighbor (2E)	$16.95	____
____	1-57248-169-2	The Power of Attorney Handbook (4E)	$19.95	____
____	1-57248-149-8	Repair Your Own Credit and Deal with Debt	$18.95	____
____	1-57248-217-6	Sexual Harassment: Your Guide to Legal Action	$18.95	____
____	1-57248-219-2	The Small Business Owner's Guide to Bankruptcy	$21.95	____
____	1-57248-168-4	The Social Security Benefits Handbook (3E)	$18.95	____
____	1-57248-216-8	Social Security Q&A	$12.95	____
____	1-57248-221-4	Teen Rights	$22.95	____
____	1-57248-236-2	Unmarried Parents' Rights (2E)	$19.95	____
____	1-57248-161-7	U.S.A. Immigration Guide (4E)	$24.95	____
____	1-57248-192-7	The Visitation Handbook	$18.95	____
____	1-57248-225-7	Win Your Unemployment Compensation Claim (2E)	$21.95	____
____	1-57248-138-2	Winning Your Personal Injury Claim (2E)	$24.95	____
____	1-57248-162-5	Your Right to Child Custody, Visitation and Support (2E)	$24.95	____
____	1-57248-157-9	Your Rights When You Owe Too Much	$16.95	____
		CALIFORNIA TITLES		
____	1-57248-150-1	CA Power of Attorney Handbook (2E)	$18.95	____
____	1-57248-151-X	How to File for Divorce in CA (3E)	$26.95	____
____	1-57071-356-1	How to Make a CA Will	$16.95	____
____	1-57248-145-5	How to Probate and Settle an Estate in California	$26.95	____
____	1-57248-146-3	How to Start a Business in CA	$18.95	____
____	1-57248-194-3	How to Win in Small Claims Court in CA (2E)	$18.95	____
____	1-57248-196-X	The Landlord's Legal Guide in CA	$24.95	____
		FLORIDA TITLES		
____	1-57071-363-4	Florida Power of Attorney Handbook (2E)	$16.95	____
____	1-57248-176-5	How to File for Divorce in FL (7E)	$26.95	____
____	1-57248-177-3	How to Form a Corporation in FL (5E)	$24.95	____
____	1-57248-203-6	How to Form a Limited Liability Co. in FL (2E)	$24.95	____
____	1-57071-401-0	How to Form a Partnership in FL	$22.95	____

Form Continued on Following Page **SUBTOTAL**

To order, call Sourcebooks at 1-800-432-7444 or FAX (630) 961-2168 (Bookstores, libraries, wholesalers—please call for discount)

Prices are subject to change without notice.

Find more legal information at: **www.SphinxLegal.com**

SPHINX® PUBLISHING ORDER FORM

Qty	ISBN	Title	Retail	Ext.
	1-57248-113-7	How to Make a FL Will (6E)	$16.95	
	1-57248-088-2	How to Modify Your FL Divorce Judgment (4E)	$24.95	
	1-57248-144-7	How to Probate and Settle an Estate in FL (4E)	$26.95	
	1-57248-081-5	How to Start a Business in FL (5E)	$16.95	
	1-57248-204-4	How to Win in Small Claims Court in FL (7E)	$18.95	
	1-57248-202-8	Land Trusts in Florida (6E)	$29.95	
	1-57248-123-4	Landlords' Rights and Duties in FL (8E)	$21.95	
		GEORGIA TITLES		
	1-57248-137-4	How to File for Divorce in GA (4E)	$21.95	
	1-57248-180-3	How to Make a GA Will (4E)	$21.95	
	1-57248-140-4	How to Start a Business in Georgia (2E)	$16.95	
		ILLINOIS TITLES		
	1-57248-244-3	Child Custody, Visitation, and Support in IL	$24.95	
	1-57248-206-0	How to File for Divorce in IL (3E)	$24.95	
	1-57248-170-6	How to Make an IL Will (3E)	$16.95	
	1-57248-247-8	How to Start a Business in IL (3E)	$21.95	
	1-57248-252-4	The Landlord's Legal Guide in IL	$24.95	
		MASSACHUSETTS TITLES		
	1-57248-128-5	How to File for Divorce in MA (3E)	$24.95	
	1-57248-115-3	How to Form a Corporation in MA	$24.95	
	1-57248-108-0	How to Make a MA Will (2E)	$16.95	
	1-57248-106-4	How to Start a Business in MA (2E)	$18.95	
	1-57248-209-5	The Landlord's Legal Guide in MA	$24.95	
		MICHIGAN TITLES		
	1-57248-215-X	How to File for Divorce in MI (3E)	$24.95	
	1-57248-182-X	How to Make a MI Will (3E)	$16.95	
	1-57248-183-8	How to Start a Business in MI (3E)	$18.95	
		MINNESOTA TITLES		
	1-57248-142-0	How to File for Divorce in MN	$21.95	
	1-57248-179-X	How to Form a Corporation in MN	$24.95	
	1-57248-178-1	How to Make a MN Will (2E)	$16.95	
		NEW YORK TITLES		
	1-57248-193-5	Child Custody, Visitation and Support in NY	$26.95	
	1-57248-141-2	How to File for Divorce in NY (2E)	$26.95	
	1-57248-249-4	How to Form a Corporation in NY (2E)	$24.95	
	1-57248-095-5	How to Make a NY Will (2E)	$16.95	
	1-57248-199-4	How to Start a Business in NY (2E)	$18.95	

Qty	ISBN	Title	Retail	Ext.
	1-57248-198-6	How to Win in Small Claims Court in NY (2E)	$18.95	
	1-57248-197-8	Landlords' Legal Guide in NY	$24.95	
	1-57071-188-7	New York Power of Attorney Handbook	$19.95	
	1-57248-122-6	Tenants' Rights in NY	$21.95	
		NEW JERSEY TITLES		
	1-57248-239-7	How to File for Divorce in NJ	$24.95	
		NORTH CAROLINA TITLES		
	1-57248-185-4	How to File for Divorce in NC (3E)	$22.95	
	1-57248-129-3	How to Make a NC Will (3E)	$16.95	
	1-57248-184-6	How to Start a Business in NC (3E)	$18.95	
	1-57248-091-2	Landlords' Rights & Duties in NC	$21.95	
		OHIO TITLES		
	1-57248-190-0	How to File for Divorce in OH (2E)	$24.95	
	1-57248-174-9	How to Form a Corporation in OH	$24.95	
	1-57248-173-0	How to Make an OH Will	$16.95	
		PENNSYLVANIA TITLES		
	1-57248-242-7	Child Custody, Visitation and Support in Pennsylvania	$26.95	
	1-57248-211-7	How to File for Divorce in PA (3E)	$26.95	
	1-57248-094-7	How to Make a PA Will (2E)	$16.95	
	1-57248-112-9	How to Start a Business in PA (2E)	$18.95	
	1-57248-245-1	The Landlord's Legal Guide in PA	$24.95	
		TEXAS TITLES		
	1-57248-171-4	Child Custody, Visitation, and Support in TX	$22.95	
	1-57248-172-2	How to File for Divorce in TX (3E)	$24.95	
	1-57248-114-5	How to Form a Corporation in TX (2E)	$24.95	
	1-57248-255-9	How to Make a TX Will (3E)	$16.95	
	1-57248-214-1	How to Probate and Settle an Estate in TX (3E)	$26.95	
	1-57248-228-1	How to Start a Business in TX (3E)	$18.95	
	1-57248-111-0	How to Win in Small Claims Court in TX (2E)	$16.95	
	1-57248-110-2	Landlords' Rights and Duties in TX (2E)	$21.95	

SUBTOTAL THIS PAGE ______

SUBTOTAL PREVIOUS PAGE ______

Shipping— $5.00 for 1st book, $1.00 each additional ______

Illinois residents add 6.75% sales tax ______

Connecticut residents add 6.00% sales tax ______

TOTAL ______

To order, call Sourcebooks at 1-800-432-7444 or FAX (630) 961-2168 (Bookstores, libraries, wholesalers—please call for discount)

Prices are subject to change without notice.

Find more legal information at: www.SphinxLegal.com